SOUTH WEST TASMANIA

Front Cover : Ketchem Island & Cox Bluff from the Amy Range
Back Cover : Forest on the side of Precipitious Bluff

SOUTH WEST TASMANIA

A guide book for bushwalkers

Fourth Edition

John Chapman

◀ *Federation Peak*

Published by
JOHN CHAPMAN
GPO Box 598D, Melbourne, Victoria 3001

FIRST PUBLISHED 1978
SECOND EDITION 1983
THIRD EDITION 1990
FOURTH EDITION 1998

National Library of Australia card number and ISBN
0 9596129 5 5

Printed by McPherson's Printing Group, Mulgrave, Victoria

While the author has endeavored to ensure that the information presented is as
up-to-date as possible, he can accept no responsibility for any loss, injury or incon-
venience sustained by any person using this book. There is a considerable amount
of danger on many of these walks from both the weather and the terrain.

For up-dates to this book either send a stamped self addressed envelope to the
above address or visit my website at
http://www.ozemail.com.au/~johnchapman

CONTENTS

PREFACE

"The remote mecca of Australian bushwalkers, Federation Peak, stood unclimbed in the Southwest until 1949, it is now visited by hundreds of people annually. The Southwest, as with the world's other wild areas is a modern Eldorado. The remaining remote and trackless country of the World Heritage Area is currently being visited by the vanguard of what will be a veritable onslaught of visitors in years to come."   Bob Brown, 1980

In 1991 the World Tourism Organisation released a study saying that tourism had become the number one industry in the world. Two of the fastest growing sectors of this gigantic industry are ecotourism and adventure travel. By the year 2000 some 650 million people will visit another country for recreation. In Australia tourism has become our major export industry with over 2.5 million visitors in 1992 and we are aiming to attract 6.5 million international visitors by the year 2000. Research by the Australian Tourist Commission confirms that Australia's greatest attraction is unspoilt nature. At the same time that we are experiencing such unprecedented growth in demand, wilderness continues to be the *"world's fastest disappearing non-renewable resource"*.

In Tasmania, the adventure travel and ecotourism industry focuses on the Tasmanian Wilderness World Heritage Area of which the Southwest is a major part. Covering more than 20% of the state it is one of the few temperate wilderness areas left in the world. It is undoubtedly one of the most beautiful landscapes on the planet - a mix of rugged mountain ranges, sparkling glacial lakes, remote windswept beaches, towering gondwanic forests, expansive buttongrass plains and delicate alpine moorlands.

But despite its rugged and often inhospitable appearance the Southwest is extremely fragile. High rainfall, steep slopes, erodible soils and delicate, slow-growing plants combine to create an environment which is highly susceptible to damage. When we add walking boots to this equation the results can be devastating. Impacts of the greatest concern include rapid deterioration of existing tracks and campsites and the growth of new unplanned tracks along many of the high exposed alpine mountain ranges. In many parts of Western Tasmania, long term damage appears to occur at extremely low usage levels. Evidence from recent controlled walker trampling trials in the Western Arthur Range suggests that walkers' pads can start to form on alpine vegetation after as few as thirty tramplings a year. Fewer than fifty tramplings a year may be sufficient to cause eventual vegetation loss and erosion. This damage is in turn compounded by the direct effects of more walkers following the newly formed pad and the natural channelling of water along the disturbed areas.

Finding a solution to these problems is now urgent. Without decisive management actions we run the risk of compromising the very values that we all cherish. In response, the Tasmanian Parks and Wildlife Service has developed a comprehensive 'Walking Track Management Strategy'. It's a bold blueprint, drawing together the whole gamut of management options for the area. The key ones include:

- a track works program involving the hardening and stabilisation of tracks, re-routing of some tracks, the introduction of 'fan out' areas and the provision of tent platforms and fly out toilets in some areas.
- an expanded education program including our *"Walking the Fine Line"* and *"Science Behind the Strategy"* videos and leaflets
- an ongoing monitoring and research program involving over 400 permanent monitoring sites, high resolution aerial photography and a series of controlled trampling trials
- the introduction of a permit system to regulate walker numbers in the most sensitive areas

Of all the recommendations contained in the Strategy, the proposal for a permit system has generated the most vigorous debate amongst the walking community. No one relishes the idea of permits and quotas in wild areas. We hear the concerns and are committed to open consultation with user groups to determine the most appropriate type of permit system for Tasmania's World Heritage Area.

Walkers have done a great job getting behind the 'Minimal Impact Bushwalking' code and the 'Fuel Stove Only' area regulations. We now hope that you will take the next step and support the 'Walking Track Management Strategy'. We believe that only a package of management initiatives, including the introduction of permits, offers a long term solution.

Enjoy this fantastic area and revel in the experience of being in the Southwest. But remember that where you are and how you walk will shape the wilderness for generations that follow. If they are to have the same chances we have, we will have to walk "softly" and in sustainable numbers through the wilderness.

Max Kitchell
Director
Parks and Wildlife Service, Tasmania

Western Tasmania World Heritage Area

INTRODUCTION

South-West Tasmania contains some of the finest and wildest bush-walking country in Australia. With its rugged coastline, open plains, thick rainforests and spectacular peaks it presents tremendous variety which has great appeal. The region contains vast tracts of true wilderness country with no roads and only a few walking tracks. It is this undeveloped nature as well as the beautiful scenery which attracts bushwalkers to seek out and experience the isolation, beauty and challenge that is to be found there.

This book describes the major tracks and walking routes in the southern half of the World Heritage Area. This covers both the South-West and the Franklin-Gordon Wild Rivers National Parks with a total area of 1,045,120ha. Within these huge parks, a large variety of both short and long walks are possible. While some day walks are described the majority of this book details lengthy walks of one week and longer.

With the isolation of the area, the extremely variable weather and roughness of some of the terrain the longer trips are not suitable for bushwalkers of limited experience. If it is your first visit , then Frenchmans Cap and the South Coast Track are highly recomended. For a second visit, South West Cape and Mt Anne are suggested.

This, the fourth edition, has seen another complete rewrite and update. The major change has been the removal of more maps which are now unnecessary with the excellent new 1:25,000 map series. You must obtain the recommended maps as the guide is designed to be used with TASMAP maps.

The guide is organized to assist in planning a trip and in executing it. However, remember that it is only a guide and not every detail is given and conditions will continue to change. In particular, management changes of the area will continue. A proposed permit system will almost certainly come into practice during the period of this edition - please check before planning trips. When walking please read and obey any signs or directions and help keep the area in its present wild state.

All walkers to wilderness areas must prepare themselves to practice Minimal Impact Bushwalking (MIB). Basically when visiting the area - cause minimum impact. Using fuel stoves instead of fires, keeping to tracks and carrying out all rubbish are some of the ways this can be done. Some places have already been altered and we must follow the MIB ethic if bushwalkers are to retain the right to visit this fine wilderness area.

BACKGROUND

HISTORY

The Tasmanian Aborigines lived in the South-West for a long period and evidence going back 30,000 years has been found in the valleys of the Franklin River and in caves to the north and east. The caves seem to have been abandoned about 10,000 years ago and the aborigines since lived beside the coast. This seems to be attributed to the spread of rainforests which supports less animals than the open plains. Even today bushwalkers will only rarely see animals in areas like the Arthur Plains. The aborigines were nomads and did have some tracks across the buttongrass plains but it seems that these were mainly used for access to the central areas of the island. One major effect that the aborigines had was to regularly burn the buttongrass to improve the chances of hunting down animals.

When Europeans came to Tasmania they established penal settlements and regarded the environment as harsh. Escapes did happen, in 1828 Goodwin managed to cross from Macquarie Harbour to the Hobart region and became the first European to cross the South-West. The next major explorer was Robinson in 1830 who set out to round up the aborigines. He mainly followed the coastline but did venture inland to climb Mt Hayes in the Western Arthurs. Five years later, one of his team, McKay, cut the Huon and Arthur Plains Tracks which are today also known as McKays Track.

The next phase of development was the whalers and piners who established themselves around Port Davey in the 1850's. By the 1870's there were permanent settlements at Port Davey as the piners explored deeper into the river systems searching for Huon Pine. As this timber grows very slowly, the supply ran out and the settlements were abandoned in the 1880's.

Inland the surveyors and track cutters remained active under the direction of the Surveyor General's Department. A railway was proposed and surveyed but thankfully was never built. Extensive burning of the country was a feature of this exploration and intense activity continued up to the end of the 1800's.

Names are usually bestowed on mountains by the first ascent party and as many of the major landmarks were still not visited at the end of the major surveying era most were as yet un-named. In 1901 T.B.Moore named the spire that had been admired from afar for so long, 'Federation Peak' after the year of Federation, even though he didn't attempt to climb it.

Mt Lot

Most of the early visitors had a job to do. In the 1870's visitors began to explore the South-West for recreation. Henry Judd was particularly notable for exploring and naming features in Cracroft and Mt Anne areas. In this period exploration was done by only a few but was to pave the way for later generations.

After the First World War interest had increased so much that the South West Expeditionary Club was formed in 1924. This was short lived but did generate further exploration. In 1929 the first ascent was made of Mt Anne and in the same year the Hobart Walking Club was formed. Clubs were planning trips well in advance and by 1939 there would be several parties on every major track during January. Most groups were following the tracks cut by the surveyors of the previous century and looked at the surrounding mountains.

In the 1930's a small family arrived in the South-West to start a tin mine. This was the King family and they were to have a major impact on visitors to the area for a long time as they were the only permanent residents. Charles King, then later his son Denis, welcomed bushwalkers at Melaleuca. Without Melaleuca and its airstrip, exploration of the South-West would have been more difficult.

Meanwhile a hardy band of bushwalkers had begun to explore the major ranges but had to wait until after the Second World War to fulfill the task. The great goal was Federation Peak which is not the highest peak in the area but is undoubtedly the most spectacular spire. Over successive summers bushwalkers from the Hobart Walking

11

Lake Fortuna

Club forged a route to the foot of the peak and almost succeeded. They freely shared their knowledge and enabled John Bechervaise to lead the first party to conquer the peak in 1949.

Attention was then turned to other areas and beautiful Lake Pedder became the main base when it was discovered airplanes could land on its hard sand. The Western Arthurs were explored and the first full traverse of the range was achieved in the early 1960's. The bushwalkers were so impressed by the beauty of this range that they named most of the features after heavenly bodies such as the planets, constellations and stars. Other major ranges were explored as it was realized what the region offered.

In 1963 the South-West Committee was formed and succeeded in having Lake Pedder declared a reserve as it was undoubtedly the most magnificient feature in the whole region. Unfortunately the HEC (Hydro Electric Commission) didn't agree and flooded the lake for a backup dam for a power scheme. As a result of the controversy the South-West National Park was declared in 1968 and has gained significant additions over the years. Controversy again raged in the 1980's when the HEC attempted to dam the Franklin and Gordon Rivers. This time, the conservationists won and significant areas were included into several new national parks. Collectively these parks form the core of the Tasmanian Wilderness World Heritage Area.

WORLD HERITAGE

The World Heritage Convention was created in 1972 by UNESCO, one of the branches of the United Nations. In 1974 Australia became the 7th country to sign the convention and today over 130 countries have signed it making it one of the worlds most signed and recognised treaties.

To be eligible for the World Heritage List, a site must be recognised as being of outstanding universal value and must satisfy at least one of a list of 11 criteria. There are four natural, six cultural and one cultural landscape criteria. World heritage covers sites like the pyramids of Egypt, the Taj Mahal and the Grand Canyon. Countries must nominate properties and these are considered at an annual meeting where proposals are rigorously assessed. Not all places that are nominated are accepted.

At present there are 552 World Heritage properties in 112 countries. Most listings are for cultural values and only 114 have natural heritage values. Australia is fairly unique having a large number of 13 properties on the list and all have been listed for their natural heritage values. Australia is also unique in that it is the only country in the world to have passed an act of parliament, the World Heritage Properties Conservation Act 1993. This legislation enabled the Federal Government to stop the dams on the Franklin and Gordon Rivers and today has implications on how the area is managed.

Comparing the Tasmanian Wilderness World Heritage Area (known locally as the WHA) with all other world heritage properties makes one realise how significant the area is. It is one of only 13 places that have satisfied all 4 natural criteria and one of only 20 places that satisfy both natural and cultural criteria. When listed it matched 7 of the 11 criteria – more than any other site in the world. The original inscription from UNESO recommended that all possible measures be taken to protect the integity of the area. Since then, only one other site in China has satisfied as many criteria for listing.

The WHA is managed by the Tasmanian Government. It covers 20% of Tasmania and it would be too much to expect the state to manage such a large area of its land as wilderness - it recieves most of its funding from the Federal Government. The biggest significance for bushwalkers is the federal legislation and the UNESCO recommendation. These basically provide directions to retain as much of the area as possible as wilderness and manage it as such. This explains why there is so much emphasis on preventing any development at all - even bushwalking pads, tracks and campsites are seen as developments. Reading the legislation, it becomes apparant why a permit and quota system are inevitable for this area as managers attempt to gain some control at retaining the existing wilderness.

GEOLOGY

The predominant rock of the South-West is PreCambrian quartzite which covers about half of the region. This very old rock has been extensively deformed by massive pressures into great waves and folds which are evident in many areas. On top of these old beds layers of sandstones and mudstones were laid down and some remnants of these remain in the Southern Ranges near La Perouse. About 380 million years ago a line of volcanoes rose along the western edge spreading debris onto the ocean floor forming the mineral rich plain from Queenstown to Low Rocky Point on the west coast.

At about the same time shallow seas covered much of the eastern side laying down beds of conglomerates and limestones. Most of the sediments had finished forming when a major upheaval occurred 165 million years ago. Deep fissures allowed massive amounts of molten rock to rise. This was released as lava on the surface and deeper down much of this spread horizontally between layers in the sediments forming massive sills. The dolerite rock that formed is evident at Mt Anne and on the Southern Ranges and may have once been much more extensive. Gradually erosion has removed most of the sediments and much of the dolerite leaving the landscape seen today.

On the surface the area can be divided into several distinct regions. The dolerite is found on top of the eastern ranges where it forms a distinctive hard red capping. Extensive screes and columnar cliffs are distinctive features. The dolerite has formed the basis of rich soils which support tall forests in the steep sided valleys.

The majority of the South-West is formed of white quartzite. This hard rock displays much evidence of the recent eras of glaciation with cirques, moraines and lakes. The rock forms the basis of poor soils and much of the area is covered with thin vegetation on the flat plains between ranges. Most of the spectacular mountains of the area, the Western Arthurs, Federation Peak and Frenchmans Cap are of quartzite.

The coastal region is interesting as the seas have risen since the ice ages to drown the southern and western coasts. The drowned valley of Port Davey is a spectacular example. On a smaller scale the Mainwaring, Lewis and Davey Rivers provide fine examples of drowned rivers where the sea extends well into them.

Drowned coastal plains are seen at Ketcham Bay, Cox Bight, New Harbour, Surprise Bay and Granite Beach. Here the ridges now form impressive headlands jutting out into the ocean. In the west these are quartzite, but further east the headlands are equally impressive dolerite ridges exposed as massive cliffs on South Cape.

VEGETATION

Due to the varied landscape and high rainfall a large variety of flora is to be found. Recent changes in climate since the ice ages mean that the vegetation is still undergoing rapid changes as to its dispersion across the area. Only 20,000 years ago much of it was under ice with the rest being a barren tundra of grasses with isolated pockets of larger species. With the warming climate these pockets formed the nucleus of the plants that cover the area today.

Many of the species present are endemic to Tasmania and some are of very ancient origin being related to the period when many of the continents were joined together as Gwondoland. The vegetation seen today can be separated into four main patterns.

(a) Wet Sedgelands. These extensive low lying plains cover about 30% of the area and the predominant plant is thick tussocky buttongrass. A great variety of species are found in narrow but very thick scrub belts that grow on the banks of the creeks which cross the plains. The plains are poorly drained and the tracks that pass along these plains are often wet and muddy.

(b) Temperate Rainforests. These thick forests can extend from sea level to high up on the ranges and are very beautiful with trees up to 100m high. Myrtle Beech is the predominant species with Tea-Tree, Blackwoods, Sassafras, Horizontal Scrub and eucalypts common. The forest floor can be open, but is usually a tangled mass of fallen trees, vines and bushes. Were it not for fire it would be reasonable to expect most of the South-West to be covered almost exclusively by rainforests. Walkers generally only enter the forests on tracks as progress otherwise is very slow.

(c) High Montane Moorland. These occur on the higher ranges where a very diverse range of hardy plants thrive. Many orchids and flowers are to be found on the very crests of the ridges and small open moors of pineapple grass, snowgrass and cushion plants exist in the most exposed places. The severe climate has helped to develop these species. The high moors provide open walking but the visitor must remember the environment here is delicate and should minimize their impact.

(d) Alpine Shrubberies. Very tough short trees and shrubs grow on the more sheltered areas of the higher ranges. Often found on precipitous slopes, scoparia and pandanni ,abound along with small forests of native pines. These small areas are very easily damaged by fires as the plants only recover slowly after burning. Where fire has occurred the shrubberies are dominated by eucalypts and scoparia. The tough alpine vegetation impedes the progress of walkers and is found on all the ranges.

Surprise Bay

WILDLIFE

Generally the South-West appears to have very little wildlife as the majority of animals are nocturnal. In fact the plains and forests support a wide variety of animals spread across the differing habitats of the area. The most common sign of life seen by bushwalkers are Wombat burrows which can be found in all areas. The other large animals are the Wallabies and Pandemelons which frequent the lightly forested regions and are rarely sighted.

Native Cats, Tiger Cats, Tasmanian Devils and Possums are the other Marsupials that are likely to be seen foraging at night. There are also a wide variety of native rats and mice that occupy the plains and forests of the area. Most visitors will only encounter these animals when they become attracted to a campsite.

On the low plains the slow moving echidna may be seen when it protects itself by displaying its sharp spines. In the rivers and lagoons platypus may sometimes be seen swimming. On the open plains yabbies are very common as evidenced by the numerous number of thumb sized burrow holes. Frogs and spiders are also common with many species being found in all areas.

Snakes are rarely seen and very rarely threatening. There are three species and as all are venomous they are best left alone. The other reptiles are lizards and skinks which are often seen sunning themselves on bare rocks in warm weather.

The most easily seen residents of the South-West are the birds. The Wedgetail Eagle and the White-Breasted Sea Eagle are the two largest and only rarely seen soaring up high. The Currawong is a common large black bird that is well known as it is fairly fearless of humans. Parrots are common in the forests where the Black Cockatoo is often found in large flocks. Smaller parrots like the Green Rosella are also often seen. The rare Orange Bellied Parrot frequents the coastal plains. Honeyeaters and waterbirds are also well represented and often seen.

CLIMATE

South-West Tasmania has a cool and changeable marine climate. It is a region of high rainfall and large temperature variations and is exposed to the full force of the prevailing westerly winds, The Roaring Forties. Precipitation is high with an annual rainfall of 3m inland and 1.2 to 2.4m along the coast. Rain falls on 250 days of each year and is fairly well spread over all seasons. Winter is typically overcast with fog, regular showers and an average of only 1½ hours of sunshine each day. Summer has no typical weather varying from hot northerly winds to periods of heavy rains and snowfalls. In a few hours the weather can change from sunshine to persistent rain and just as quickly fine up again. Summer has a sunshine average of 7 out of the 16 hours of daylight each day.

Late summer is the best time to visit this area. January often has an unstable weather pattern and the best chance of fine weather is during February and March. Then, the generally mild (sometimes hot) weather provides ideal walking conditions but even then the winds can swiftly bring in cold, wet weather, with snowfalls and high winds. Walkers can be prevented from any movement for several days, especially in the higher ranges. Down on the plains the weather is less severe but the creeks and rivers rise to flood level rapidly and all parties must be prepared to wait for them to subside.

In other seasons, fine weather is rare. The prevailing westerly winds bring rain, hail and snowfalls with snow often lying on the ranges in winter. Crossing the swollen rivers and creeks can be difficult. Only very experienced parties familiar with snow camping and river crossings should attempt a trip. Even these parties may be foiled. Snow cover is extremely variable from very little to snow right down to sea level.

The weather may appear bleak but in fact during summer it is often fine. Be warned and well prepared, for the infamous bad weather does occur and even in summer can last for several weeks. People have died from exposure in the past and help is often many days away.

PREPARATION AND PLANNING

To walk through this large undeveloped area of Australia careful preparation and planning is essential. This will reduce the risks involved and improve the chances of an enjoyable visit. The well prepared party will have fewer problems if they are ready to cope with all conditions from heat waves to snow storms.

Party Size. The minimum recommended size for safety is four people. The reason for this is that if help is needed, then two can walk out while one remains to look after the patient. Groups smaller than four are not encouraged and if contemplating a very small party size, then prior experience in the area is considered essential.

The maximum party size should be held to six people (or three tents) as campsites are generally very small and of poor quality. Larger parties will find themselves often camping on soggy or uneven ground exposed to the full force of the weather. This is hardly the ideal way to enjoy the area. The only real exception to this is the South Coast Track where with the abundance of well used, large campsites, a party size of twelve can be acceptable.

Maps. No party should walk in this area without carrying the appropriate maps. The TASMAP series is the best available and is available in two series. The topographic series show vegetation density and are the most useful to walkers but are not regularly revised. The following TASMAPS cover all the routes in this book.

- TASMAP 1:100,000 Old River, Wedge, Huon, Port Davey, Olga, Spero, Cape Sorrell, Franklin, South East Cape, South West Cape, South Coast Walks
- TASMAP 1:25,000 See the map notes for each walk.
- Most bushwalking shops and specialist map shops in south-eastern Australia stock TASMAPS. Thay can also be purchased by mail order from TASMAP in Hobart (p 29).

Each route description in the text details the required maps. In addition, maps are provided in this book when the TASMAP series are inadequate for navigation. The map references given apply to the grid on the TASMAP series as well as the maps in this book. The maps in the text are not intended to be used on their own.

Another most useful map is a road map to Tasmania showing access into the South-West. Sitting on a peak in clear weather, a road map can assist in identifying peaks in the distance.

Equipment. The walker venturing into the South-West must be completely self sufficient. Good equipment in good order is essential at all times of the year. Gear lists vary with the individual and evolve through experience. The following lists are offered as suggestions which have satisfied several very experienced walkers in the South-West. Undoubtedly, other walkers would suggest some amendments to the list. The equipment listed is that required for a summer walk in the area.

Personal Equipment (to carry or wear at all times)

Parka (Blizzard Jacket)	Essential, must be completely waterproof and windproof with a hood.
Overpants	Must be waterproof and fit over trousers.
Trousers	Loose fitting wool pants or nordic ski pants.
Light Shirt	A light shirt or blouse.
Jacket	Warm long sleeved wool shirt or a synthetic fibrepile or bunting jacket are ideal.
Mittens or gloves	Should be carried. If lost, wool socks can be used as temporary mittens.
Hat or balaclava	A well fitting balaclava is best.
Boots or runners	Must be comfortable and provide good foot support. If using runners, carry a spare pair.
Gaiters	Very useful in the scrub and mud.
Waterbottle	One litre is suggested for carrying water for use during the day.
Notebook & Pencil	For writing messages and taking notes.
Whistle	Should be carried at all times.
Pocket Knife	Useful.
Maps & Guidebook	Keep handy in map case or plastic bags.
Compass	Each walker should carry their own and know how to use it.
First Aid Kit	Personal and general needs such as band aids, elastoplast, sunscreen etc.
High Energy Food	Carry in pockets for regular consumption, sweets, chocolate, glucose, etc.

Personal Equipment (to carry in the pack)

Pack	Durability is the main requirement, but it also helps if it is waterproof. There are many suitable designs, take a good one and make sure it is large enough.
Pack Liner	Plastic bags or a waterproof pack liner should be used to keep gear dry. Carry spare plastic bags.

Sleeping Bag	As the temperature occasionally falls below freezing in summer a good warm sleeping bag is essential. Superdown or featherdown have the best warmth to weight ratio and are the usual choice. Some synthetics are suitable but bulky when packed, a problem on longer walks.
Innersheet	Keeps that expensive sleeping bag cleaner.
Sleeping Mat	Improves sleeping comfort.
Spare Clothing	A complete change of light clothing should be kept dry at all times for night and emergency use.
Shorts & Light Shirt	Useful when the weather is hot.
Socks	Several woollen pairs should be carried and be regularly washed during the trip.
Underwear	Normal underwear is suitable. Thermal underwear is popular in cold weather.
Torch & Candles	Take spare globes and batteries.
Utensils	Mug, plate, knife, fork and spoon.
Camera & Film	Optional, use plastic bags to keep dry.
Sandshoes	Light spare footwear for around camp and in case boots fail.
Toilet Gear	Personal hygiene items
Small towel, soap and toothbrush	Try not use any soap. Take biodegradable soap but use sparely as it does pollute water.
Toilet Paper	Uses are obvious, dispose in toilet or bury it.
Nylon Cord	20m of light cord is useful for tent guys, shoe laces, clothes line, etc.
Book, Cards & Games	Optional, useful when tent-bound to pass the time.
Food	See separate note (p 24)

Party equipment

Tent	A good tent is essential. Double skin nylon tents designed for winter conditions are ideal. Sewn in floors and storm guys are needed and snow pegs are useful in soft muddy ground.
Groundsheet	A 2.5 x 2m light waterproof sheet is useful as all tent floors leak.
Water bucket or Winecask Inner	Handy for collecting and carrying water for camp.
Billycans	Several will be needed for the party.
Billygrips	Saves burnt fingers.
Boot Proofing	For application during the trip.
Stove	Essential for all walks, campfires are banned.

Fuel Bottle	
	A leak proof bottle for the stove fuel.
Pot Scourer	Carry in a plastic bag.
Mending Kit	Pack and clothes may require repair. Soft wire, scissors, needles and thread safety pins, rivets, screws and nails are useful.
Rope	20m of 6 or 7mm climbing rope is desirable on several of the high level walks for packhauling and as a safety line for river crossings.
First Aid Kit	Essential, see separate note.
Trowel	Essential for toilet waste disposal.

Winter Equipment. In addition to the summer list the following are also necessary. Note that even in winter there can be mild weather so retain some light clothing in your pack.

Jacket	Either add a vest or use a heavier garment.
Dark Goggles or Glasses	Needed in snow conditions to prevent snow blindness.
Boot	Built-in padded insulation is highly desirable.

First Aid. As the party can be many days away from help a comprehensive first aid kit should be carried. At least one member of the party should be trained in its use. One of the first aid manuals should be carried.

Food. As the party will be walking for many days it is very important to plan a balanced diet. It is also desirable that the food taken be light-weight, have high energy value, be easy to prepare, be tasty and appealing, and keep well in wet as well as hot weather. Also, morale can be kept up by having a variety from day to day and by the inclusion of a few treats which should be saved for wet, miserable days or special occasions.

To keep weight down select foods that contain little or no water. Allow between 700 to 900g of food per person per day. The following list indicates the large variety that can be easily obtained and is not meant to be comprehensive.

Oats (porridge)	Muesli	Flour
Damper	Freeze Dried Meals	Foil Sealed Meals
Pasta	Rice & Noodles	Dried Vegetables
Powdered Potato	Packet Soups	Egg Powder
Powdered Milk	Nuts	Cheese
Dried Biscuits	Sweet Biscuits	Rye Bread
Lunch Spreads	Cabana	Salami
Butter/Margarine	Dried Fruit	Custard Powder
Instant Pudding	Chocolate	Sweet Bars
Pancake Mixes	Packet Desert Mixes	Fruit Cake
Coffee	Tea	Sugar

Water. There is usually plenty of water around on the plains where creeks are regularly crossed. Up on the ranges water is sometimes difficult to find. A one litre water bottle should be carried for use during the day. Usually there is water near the regular campsites and a water bucket or wine cask is a useful addition. Generally most water is safe to drink - if there is any doubt then boil it for 5 minutes first.

Airdrops. No airdrops are allowed within the National Park. Food can be flown into Melaleuca and left there for collection. Parties that want to have a ready food supply will have to plan their trips accordingly so that food can be collected there. If supplies are being flown in they need to be delivered to the airline at least two weeks prior to the date they are required. Supplies can often be taken in on one days notice but do not rely on this. All bags and wrapping should be clearly labelled with name and address, expected date of collection and an expiry date after which anyone may use the food. Unfortunately, food supplies are occasionally opened by unscrupulous people - any such incident should be reported to the police. To prevent such events, parties are encouraged to fly in with their food, thus enabling it to be securely stored for later recovery rather than leave it beside the airstrip in the shelter hut.

Tas Air and Par Avion (p 28) are light plane companies that fly supplies and people into Melaleuca. It is advisable to make advance bookings for both supply drops and party flights.

Food can also be delivered to Scotts Peak, Cockle Creek and Lune River via the regular TWT bus services (p 26). If the party misses the pre-arranged day they normally bring it in again on the next scheduled service.

For parties walking along the west coast, food drops can be arranged with Wilderness Air (p 28). See walk notes (p 95) for details of suitable sites.

Trip Registration. Due to the large number of walkers entering Tasmania's wilderness the registration system has now been changed. Do not register with the police. Do not rely on information left with rangers or the proposed permit system for initiating a search.

Each party should fill out a detailed itinerary and leave it with a responsible relative or friend. The information should include the leaders name, address and phone numbers, all party member names and an intended trip plan. Include the starting date and expected completion date along with the date when a rescue should be initiated. Other details should include the number of days food carried. The person holding this information must be aware that it is their responsibility to forward the information to the Tasmanian Police if necessary.

Fill out the registration books at the start of walk, any log books along the route and remember to de-register at the end. These books are not regularly checked but are useful in pin-pointing locations of all groups once Search and Rescue has been alerted that a party is overdue. Also during bushfires, the books can help to locate parties who could be in danger from fires or backburns. Remember the books are no substitute for leaving your itinerary with someone reliable.

Transport. Previously this was a major problem when planning a trip into the South-West, but now several companies provide regular transport during the summer into the area. In other seasons chartered bookings only are taken and these must be made in advance. All addresses have been grouped together at the end of this chapter.

(a) **Tasmanian Wilderness Travel (TWT).** Based in Launceston, they provide a regular minibus service on Saturday, Sunday, Tuesday and Thursday to Scotts Peak Dam and Mt Anne from early December until Easter. They also operate another service on Monday, Wednesday and Friday to Cockle Creek over the same period. They also operate a coach all year from Hobart to Quenstown along the Lyell Highway on Tuesday, Thursday, Saturday and Sunday. In addition, by booking a charter, they can collect or deliver parties to any other road access points.

They can arrange accommodation in Hobart at reasonable prices, provide gear storage at the Transit Centre (during office hours) and sell most liquid fuels (it is advised to order fuel when booking). If you have made a booking and leave the South-West by another means (eg with other walkers) then it is requested that you inform TWT. This may prevent an unnecessary search for your party.

At times there have been complaints about TWT and often the problem has been a lack of understanding about the service. The timetable is approximate - be ready at least 20 minutes before the scheduled time. If you have booked a seat, they do not wait if you are not there - bushwalkers often modify trips. The drivers often inquire about the whereabouts of groups who missed the last service - they do care, but cannot wait for a half hour when parties could be one or two days late. Its also important to realise the services run on demand - no bookings and the service might get cancelled. Breakdowns can also happen and the route with the smallest number of bookings is the one that will miss out that day. Over 20 years I have come to regard TWT as very reliable - there has been the rare problem which is often caused by passengers who have not booked crowding the service. Overall, I have had more problems getting to Tasmania than with TWT services.

(b) **Tas Air.** This small light plane company operates fairly regular flights from Hobart to Melaleuca during the summer, according to demand and the weather. They are based at Cambridge Airport near Hobart. Food supplies can be taken in with 2 weeks notice during summer. Due to supplies being occasionally pilfered it is suggested to fly in with supplies, hide them for later collection and then walk out. They hold stocks of stove fuels - order when booking flights.

(c) **Par Avion.** Another light plane company based near Hobart that can be chartered to fly to Melaleuca. Services provided are the same as for Tas Air including stove fuel. Both companies can also be chartered to fly to Moores Valley on the west coast (p 98).

(d) **Wilderness Air.** Based at Strahan on the west coast this company operates several light sea planes that can be chartered. As the planes require an open body of flat water for a runway they can be used for many interesting destinations. On the west coast; the lower Franklin River, Hells Gates, Birches Inlet, Hibbs Lagoon and Bond Bay are good landing sites. Virtually anywhere around Bathurst Harbour, Lake Pedder and Lake Gordon can be accessed. Bookings are essential as the planes are heavily used for tourist flights and some destinations within the World Heritage Area require prior approval.

Transport and Accommodation. The Tasmanian Tourist Bureau publish a regular, free newspaper called Tasmanian Travelways. This is a very useful guide for transport services to and around Tasmania and also includes a guide to accommodation, including prices. It is well worth obtaining although prices are often out-of-date.

Addresses. The following list should be helpful to any party that is planning a walk into this area.

Tasmanian Wilderness Travel   (details p 26)
P.O. Box 2053, Launceston, 7250
Phone (03) 6334 4442, Fax (03) 6334 2029
Intenet   http://www.tassie.net.au/wildtour
> Bus transport to Scotts Peak, Cockle Creek and Frenchmans Cap Track. Other places by charter.

TasAir P/L (Cambridge Airport)   (details p 27)
GPO Box 451E, Hobart 7001
Phone (03) 6248 5088, Fax (03) 6248 5528
> Flights to Melaleuca and scenic joy flights over the WHA.

Par Avion (Cambridge Airport)   (details p 27)
GPO Box 324, Rosny Park 7018
Phone (03) 6248 5390, Fax (03) 6248 5117
Internet: http://www.tassie.net.au/~paravion/
> Flights to Melaleuca and scenic joy flights over the WHA.

Wilderness Air (Strahan)   (details p 27)
PO Box 92, Strahan 7468
Phone (03) 6471 7280, Fax (03) 6471 7303
> Sea plane charter on the west coast.

Tasmanian Expeditions
110 George St, Launceston 7250
Phone (03) 6334 3477 or 1800 030 230, Fax (03) 6334 3463
Internet: http://www.tassie.net.au/tas_ex/
> Tours along South Coast Track and Franklin River rafting.

Craclair Tours
PO Box 516, Devonport 7310
Phone (03) 6424 7833, Fax (03) 6424 7833
Internet: http://www.ozemail.com.au/~craclair/
> Tours to Frenchmans Cap, has been running tours for 20 years.

Lake Oberon

Parks and Wildlife Service
134 Macquarie St, Hobart 7000
Phone (03) 6233 6191, Fax (03) 6223 8765
Internet: http://www.parks.tas.gov.au/
> Advice for current regulations and permits. For specific tracks they can mail sheets titled 'Track Notes' - these are not descriptions of the walks, instead they describe the latest regulations and recommended changes to tracks and campsites. Also they supply educational videos and supporting material. The web site has a wealth of general information that supplements this book.

TASMAP Centre, 134 Macquarie St, Hobart
GPO Box 44A, Hobart 7001
Phone (03) 6233 3382, Fax (03) 6233 2158
> Produce excellent contour maps and aerial photographs.

WALKING INFORMATION

When visiting this large region there is a simple code of ethics to follow which will reduce your impact and increase your appreciation of this fine wilderness. Observing these will also improve the safety of the group. Apart from the human element there are also some special climatic conditions which the party may not have encountered before. Floods and snowfall often occur in summer, so with proper preparation and the use of commonsense the danger of these conditions can be reduced.

Entry Fees and Permits. An entry fee now applies to all Nationals Parks in Tasmania. For short visits, the fee is $3 per day per person. For the trips in this guide the $12 Backpacker Pass is recommended as it provides 2 month entry to all National Parks for one person. For local walkers, the $42 Annual Pass for one vehicle to all parks will probably be the best choice.

At present no permits are required to walk in the area covered by this guide. A detailed permit system has been proposed (mid 1998) and is currently being discussed and revised. It is expected that permits will be needed for all walks in this guide by the year 2000 (contact parks, p 29). The current proposal is free permits (you already pay an entry fee) and a limit on numbers of bushwalkers will apply to most walks. It is proposed to have quotas on both total yearly numbers and also weekly totals. An obvious benefit will be a reduction in crowding at campsites; on the negative side you might have to change your holidays to a period when a permit is available. Overall the permit system is not intended to reduce the walking opportunities and a lot of public consultation has been done to create a system that hopefully, will be reasonably fair to bushwalkers.

National Park Management. All the major bushwalking routes are now being actively managed.This means that tracks are being repaired if necessary, campsites hardened and routes altered. The routes will not be fixed to eliminate mud and rough walking conditions. Current policy is to only make changes when the environment is being unacceptably altered by bushwalkers. Installing water bars, moving tracks onto harder surfaces like rocks and providing board walks across marshy ground are all part of this policy. In some areas, the rangers are trying to not make changes by introducing a fan-out policy. If this prevents a muddy track forming then they will not need to build walkways and most walkers would prefer this. When you encounter signposts giving directions like fan-out or track closures of short-cuts please follow the directions. The less impact we make overall will encourage management to not introduce severe quotas on walking numbers. At present they are trying to allow as many as possible to visit the region while keeping the quality of the wilderness intact.

Rubbish. Rubbish has always a problem and the rule here is simple; carry in, carry out. To reduce litter, airdrops of food supplies are not permitted within the South-West National Park except at Melaleuca where planes can land.

A very visible rubbish problem is also caused by those who carry foam mats on the outside of their packs. These get shredded in scrub and you often find you are following trails of blue and green foam along the routes. My advice is to put the mat inside your pack - put it in first, don't roll it, instead use it as a liner and pack your gear inside it. This way it takes up little space, helps to keep water away from your contents and also cushions your gear from damage.

General Hygiene. Illness due to contaminated water supplies is now a common problem in the bush. All walkers should be aware of this and act accordingly. At a campsite, first look for a toilet and use it if it exists. If there is no toilet then select a site at least 100 metres away from all campsites and water sources (preferably downstream), dig a hole 150mm deep and most importantly cover with soil. A small

trowel should be carried for this purpose. Always wash or swim downstream of all watering sites and please don't use soap for washing; sand or a scourer is just as effective a pot cleaner and pollution free. All cooking gear should be washed well away from streams to prevent food scraps polluting the water.

Fire Safety. The entire World Heritage Area has now been declared a 'Fuel Stove Only' area. You must bring all of your stove fuel with you; a 'stove' that burns sticks and twigs inside a container is considered to be a campfire. Campfires are now only allowed at a couple of designated sites where a fireplace is provided. Fuel stoves have made campfires unnecessary as they are much quicker to use and do not create large environmental impacts. Campfires did not just leave piles of ashes or occasionally escape and create a bushfire – they also caused the removal of most bushes and plants around campsites.

Huts and Campsites. Huts in this area are very few and far between and as a result all parties must carry tents. The only huts in the South-West are found at Melaleuca and Mt Eliza. At other places there once was some three sided shelters but they have now all been removed. This guide describes one hut serviced walk, Frenchmans Cap which has two huts. On that walk you should carry tents but use the huts if space is available.

South Coast Campsite

When using a hut or campsite, animosity sometimes exists between parties. All walkers have equal rights to each place. Naturally early arrivals choose the most comfortable sites but they have no right to take over all the amenities and should leave space for others. Most late arrivals are most appreciative of a little help and many friendships have resulted from common sharing.

Another problem is between groups who have different sleeping patterns. Some go to bed at sunset while others sit around for hours talking, then in the morning some are up at dawn when others wish to sleep in. If you find that your camp life is vastly different to that of others then set up your next camp well apart. If necessary, discuss it calmly to make others aware of the problem and negotiate different camp locations. Please remember that each person has come for a different reason and wants a different experience. The proposed permit system should reduce this conflict as it is designed to reduce crowding on the most popular walks.

River Crossings. Even in the summer months rivers can flood especially along the South Coast Track and the West Coast. Rivers can rise overnight and it is a good policy to cross and camp on the opposite bank at all large streams. If a river is flooded it is best to camp and wait for it to drop until it is at a safe level to cross. Often, rivers drop dramatically overnight, at the worst it involves a wait of only one or two days.

Snowfall and Exposure. It is a great surprise to many that even during the summer months low temperatures and snowfalls do occur. Such cold wet conditions can easily bring on exposure and well equiped parties with warm clothing, extra food and a flexible itinerary that allow them to wait several days for better weather, will minimise the risks. There are several excellent publications dealing with the risks of exposure.

Rescues. The South West is a remote area. Often the quickest route out is the way you have just walked. For this reason, rescue involves commonsense and self initiative. The party should carefully plan emergency exit routes and action that can be taken. Other walkers in the area should be informed of the situation. Sometimes the solution is simply several days rest to cure a minor ailment. However, if the patient cannot continue then help must be sought by the quickest possible means. Always leave at least one fit, healthy people with the patient and make sure that they are aware it could take up to a week before help is obtained. For these reasons a comprehensive first aid kit is a necessity and current first aid training is desirable. All walkers should be fit and healthy before entering the area.

THE WALKING ROUTES

Within this large undeveloped region there are an amazing variety of walking visits possible. For the very inexperienced or those with limited time there is a range of one day and weekend walks to choose from. For those with more experience and time the long trips of a week or longer are highly recommended.

For a first visit the long easy tracks of the South Coast (p 40), Port Davey (p 58), Frenchmans Cap (p 180) and the Huon and Arthur Plains Tracks (p 54) are suggested. With previous off track experience South West Cape (p 78), the top section of the West Coast (p 95) and the Mt Anne Circuit (p 108) are also excellent to tackle for a first or second visit. To highly experienced walkers the full West Coast (p 95) and the high level traverses of the Western Arthurs (p 118), Federation Peak (p 144), Precipitous Bluff (p 66) and the Frankland Range (p 173) provide rugged walking and spectacular scenery.

All parties should be aware that most of the high level routes involve packhauling and are subject to severe weather changes that can keep parties storm bound in tents for days. For walkers of limited experience, a professional guided trip with Tasmanian Expeditions or Craclair Tours is suggested (p 28).

Walking Times. The times given are for average experienced walkers. They do not allow for long rests, lunch stops, sightseeing and sidetrips and these extras must be added on to the times. Most groups use between 1 to 2 hours extra each day. The times are based on the authors personal experience with comments from other bushwalkers. As conditions vary so much the times are given as a guide only. In good conditions they can be beaten and on the other end, in poor weather loaded with 10 days food many walkers will take longer than suggested.

This is the biggest criticism this guide recieves. Personally at the start of trips I often take longer than the longest time but by the end of the trip I am taking less than the shortest time as I become fitter and my pack gets lighter. Overall I take an average from those I meet. If I provided the full possible range then times of 1 to 6 hours and 3 to 12 hours would appear and be virtually useless.

Interpreting the Notes. In this guide, track is used where an easy to follow trail exists. Usually tracks are marked by stakes, tape markers or cairns and they are often of a poor rough standard with mud, tree roots and an occasional scramble common. A route is described

Federation Peak from the Eastern Arthurs

where no consistent track exists and parties need to navigate carefully to follow the route. Many routes have small sections of well defined track through the awkward areas then are open and undefined elsewhere. Note that as the routes become more used they gradually become tracks. Notes for the reverse direction are shown in italics when necessary.

Day Trips. While these walks only venture a short way into this area they display the full diversity of the South West.

- Junction Creek. Sheltered walking along the lightly forested hills near Scotts Peak; 3½ to 5 hours return; see p 58.
- Lake Judd. A pleasant sheltered walk starting from Red Tape Creek; 4 to 6 hours return; see p 117.
- Schnells Ridge. Excellent views of the Western Arthurs and Anne area starting at Red Tape Creek; 5 to 7 hours return; see p 117.
- Mt Eliza. A steep climb for good views of the Lake Pedder impoundment; 4 to 6 hours return; see p 108.
- Mt Anne. A very long day to the highest mountain in the South West; 8 to 10 hours return; see p 108.

- Mt Sprent. A steep climb near Strathgordon for excellent views of that area; 5 to 7 hours return; see p 173.
- South Cape Bay. Sheltered flat walking to a grand ocean beach, start at Cockle Creek; 4 to 6 hours return, see p 40.
- Blakes Opening. Sheltered walking along a good track in thick forest beside the Huon River; 3 to 5 hours return; see p 54.

Two and Three Day Walks. Not all walkers can afford to use a week or longer for walking. With only two or three days there is a limited range of trips to be undertaken.

- Mt Anne. An easy two day trip camping at Shelf Camp and return via the same route; see p 108.
- Mt Anne Circuit. A hard two days or three medium days on an exposed high level circuit; see p 108.
- Lake Cygnus. A long two days to give a brief sample of the Western Arthurs, return via the same route; see p 118.
- Huon and Arthur Plains Tracks. Two long or three medium days along the Huon River, sheltered walking; see p 54.
- South Cape Rivulet. An enjoyable two day return walk on the South Coast, see p 40.
- The Hippo. A high level two day return walk on the Southern Ranges near Lune River; see p 66.
- Mt La Perouse. A high level hard two or medium three day return walk on the southern ranges near Lune River; see p 66.
- Frenchmans Cap Return. A medium walk returning along the same track. Hard 2 to easy 4 day walk; see p 180.

Extended Walks. These trips are the best way to really appreciate this fine area. They are the most popular of all the trips done and vary from 4 to 14 days in length. Within this time period most areas of the South West can be visited. With walks of this length the time taken varies considerably with party fitness and the prevailing weather conditions hence the variations given below. Many route variations are possible from those listed.

- Mt Anne Circuit. Use 2 to 4 days to relax and explore the circuit of this remarkable area; see p 108.
- Frenchmans Cap Circuit. Follow track to the Cap then past Irenabyss to Victoria Pass. Allow 4 to 6 days; see p 180.
- South Coast Track to Melaleuca. An easy walk along well formed tracks. Fly out from Melaleuca. Allow 5 to 8 days; see p 40.
- South Coast Track to Melaleuca then the Port Davey Track. An easy walk on wet tracks. Allow 8 to 12 days; see p 40 & 58.
- South West Cape Circuit. Fly in to Melaleuca then easy walking in open country by the coast. Allow 7 to 9 days ; see p 78.

- Cape Sorrell to Hibbs Lagoon. An easy coastal traverse in untracked country on the west coast. Allow 5 to 6 days; see p 95.
- Birches Inlet to Port Davey. Follow a bombardier track to Low Rocky Point then untracked country along the coast. Allow 8 to 12 days; see p 95.
- Federation Peak via the Eastern Arthurs. Walk from Scotts Peak Dam via Cracroft Crossing and then along the Eastern Arthurs and return via same route. A high level walk on very rough tracks. Allow 7 to 10 days for the return trip; see p 146.
- Federation Peak via Farmhouse Creek then along the Eastern Arthurs and out either the Huon or Arthur Plains Track. While this is a through route it is not as exciting as walking the Eastern Arthers twice. Allow 6 to 9 days; see p 156 & 146.
- Western Arthurs Traverse. The traverse of this range is the most spectacular walk in the South West and also one of the most popular. A varied high level route. Allow 9 to 12 days; see p 118.
- Precipitous Bluff Traverse. A high level traverse across the southern ranges then continue along the South Coast Track in either direction. Very varied with open moors, thick scrub then the coastal track. Allow 8 to 10 days; see p 66.
- Frankland Range Traverse. Another high level traverse along the Lake Pedder impoundment. Allow 9 to 12 days; see p 173.
- Hibbs Lagoon to Low Rocky Point then north to Birches Inlet. A difficult coastal traverse on the west coast. Allow 14 to 16 days; see p 95.

Multiple Week Visits. Some parties enjoy walking in this area so much that they remain in it for several weeks combining several major routes together. This involves some careful pre-planning to positon food caches at suitable locations. The suggestions given here are the more popular combinatons.

- Western Arthurs and Federation Peak. To walk these together it is best to leave food at Cracroft Crossing or Pass Creek. Most parties carry very heavy loads from Scotts Peak to put in the food dump and visit Federation Peak first. Allow 2 to 3 weeks.
- South Coast Track, South West Cape then along the Port Davey Track to Scotts Peak Dam. An easy long trip with food being flown in to Melaleuca by light aeroplane. Allow about 3 weeks.
- Precipitous Bluff then on to Melaleuca and the Port Davey Track to visit the Western Arthurs. Another good combination for those who like variety. Food is easily arranged at Melaleuca (by air) and at Scotts Peak Dam with the minibus services. Allow 3½ to 4½ weeks.
- West Coast Traverse. From Cape Sorrell follow the coast south to Port Davey, fly out or head east to the Port Davey Track to Scotts Peak. Allow 3 to 4½ weeks; see p 95.

MAP INDEX AND LEGEND

MAP INDEX

MAP LEGEND

Road . . . .
Walking Track . . . .
Walking Route . . . .
Signpost . . . .   sp
Railway (abandoned) . . . .
Cliff . . . .
Sink hole . . . .
Lakes . . . .
Stream . . . .
Waterfall . . . .
Hut . . . .
Peak . . . .
Campsite . . . .
Page Reference to Adjoining Map   96

Grid lines are the same as the TASMAP series.

All heights in metres.

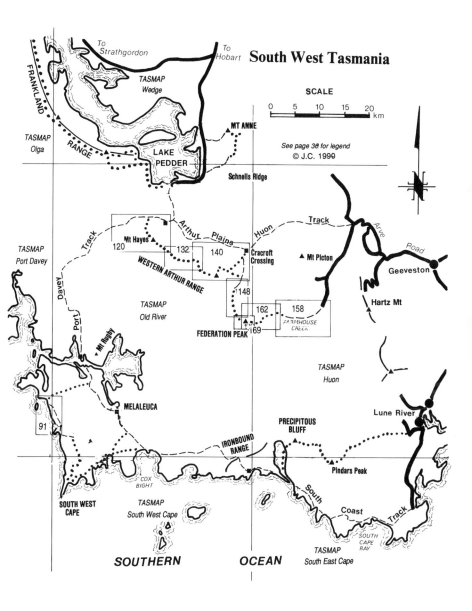

South West Tasmania

SCALE

0 5 10 15 20 km

See page 38 for legend
© J.C. 1990

SOUTH COAST TRACK

This very popular walk traverses the magnificent south coast of Tasmania from Cockle Creek to Melaleuca at Port Davey. Often it is combined with the Port Davey Track to give a great 10 days plus of walking. This combined walk is often referred to by other writers as the South West Track. The track is well marked and easily followed although it is rather muddy. A track reconstruction program has improved the conditions encountered. It passes along wild ocean beaches, through rain forests, over high ridges and along buttongrass plains forming an easy long walk that is hard to beat. It is the best introductory walk to this area.

The track also forms an access route for those going to Precipitious Bluff and South West Cape. The track was created as an escape route for shipwrecked sailors in 1905 and was recut in 1915, 1930, 1946 and 1966. The present track is maintained by the Parks & Wildlife Service.

Maps.   TASMAP 1:100,000 South Coast Walks.
TASMAP 1:100,000 Old River, South West Cape, South East Cape.
TASMAP 1:25,000 Cox, Prion, Recherche.
The track is clearly marked on the above maps. The South Coast Walks is the most up-to-date and recommended.

Standard. Although this track is fairly easy for the South-West it should be recognised that the party will be away from civilization for at least 5 days. It is desirable to have previous bushwalking experience at carrying a self sufficient pack for several days. Some parties underestimate the standard of this walk. The track itself is easy to follow.

Notes.
- There is a high level section over the Ironbound Range which is very exposed. All parties should be prepared to wait out any storms before attempting to cross the range.
- After heavy rains the creeks and rivers can rise very rapidly and flood, even in mid-summer. All walkers should be prepared to wait until the water level drops. It is advised that when camping beside a major stream, cross and camp on the other bank as flooding can occur overnight. Be aware that a stream can flood even though it has not rained on the coast.
- Several sections of the track are often very wet and muddy.

South Cape Bay

- Rowboats are provided for crossing New River Lagoon. Please leave one good boat tied up on each side at all times.
- There are plenty of established campsites along the coast. Use an existing campsite - do not create new tent sites. All the major campsites have pit toilets – they are not always obvious so look first before heading to dig a hole.
- The track is now a 'Fuel Stove Only' area. Campfires are now banned except at Surprise Bay and Little Deadmans Bay.
- No airdrops of supplies are allowed along the track. Airdrops or flights by light airplane can be arranged for Melaleuca (p 27).
- Tents are definitely required - the only hut is at Melaleuca.

Walking Times. See p 34 for an explanation of the section times - remember to add extra time for stops.

(a) Cockle Creek to Melaleuca (or Cox Bight) requires 5 days of walking. It is recommended to take 7 to 9 days. This allows extra time to explore the coastline and laze on the beaches; too many parties race along the track without having a good look at the area. Some extra food should always be carried in case of floods or storms. The track itself is easy to follow and often very muddy.

(b) For parties intending to visit Precipitous Bluff, Prion Beach can be reached from either Cockle Creek or Melaleuca in 2 to 4 days.

(c) From Cockle Creek, South Cape Rivulet is either a long return daytrip or an easy 2 day return walk.

(d) South Cape Bay is an easy return daytrip from Cockle Creek.

Access. (a) **East end.** Follow the highway south from Hobart to Lune River. Pass through Lune River and follow the signposted roads south, a further 18km to Cockle Creek. This road is gravel, in reasonable condition and ends at the bridge at Cockle Creek. Camp in the designated areas. Use water from the taps, the creek is usually brackish.

During the summer access is easy with a TWT bus service operating from Hobart and Geeveston on Monday, Wednesday and Friday (p 26). At other times of the year a bus runs to Dover, about 25km from Cockle Creek and it is preferable to hire a taxi or a minibus from TWT (p 26).

(b) **West end.** Melaleuca can be reached by light aircraft (p 27), by boat or the Port Davey Track (p 58). There is an open hut at Melaleuca for walkers to use.

1. Cockle Creek — South Cape Rivulet
11km, 3½ to 4½ hours

Easy flat walking on a constructed track crosses the plains, then the beaches and rocks on the coast are traversed to the Rivulet. The track is easy to follow.

From the bridge at Cockle Creek, follow the vehicle track on the south shore upstream for 100m to a closed gate. Pass through the gate into a clearing and follow the foot track to an information shelter. After filling out the log book follow the well defined track south-west over a low rise through light forest. The track then follows the southern edge of Blowhole Valley for 5km to Jeephead Camp beside a creek (868716).

Follow the track south-west to South Cape Bay, turn west along the cliff tops and descend the timber staircase to the sand. *(To parties travelling east, from the end of the sand (856713) climb the staircase. Follow the cut track parallel to the coast for a further 200m then turn inland north-east towards Blowhole Valley.)*

Follow the sand beach, west to Lion Rock and just past this is a rocky wall forming an obstacle. If the tide is low climb over a small saddle and scramble along the rocks under the wall to the next beach. If the tide is high use the signposted inland track which climbs high above the wall and over Coal Bluff providing good views. Rough scrambling along the rocks under Coal Bluff leads to a sandy beach to

Granite Beach

meet the other end of the inland track. Walk west along the sand, climb over the small headland and along the next beach to South Cape Rivulet.

Campsites :
- Jeephead Camp (868716). Good shelter and fair water 1km north of South Cape Bay.
- Lion Rock (852717). A few sheltered sites cut into the scrub near the second small creek east of Lion Rock.
- South Cape Headland (832723). On ridge 1km east of South Cape Rivulet. Water 10 minutes walk in either direction along the beaches.
- South Cape Rivulet (826723). Best campsites are on the east bank. Water from the lagoon which is sometimes brackish.

2. South Cape Rivulet — Granite Beach 8km, 5 to 7 hours

A fairly long section with poor intermediate campsites and few creeks - carry water for the day. It involves a gradual slow climb through the rainforest onto the South Cape Range for a superb view then a steep descent to Granite Beach. The track is easy to follow and often muddy through the rainforest.

Wade South Cape Rivulet to the west bank. This can be difficult at high tide or after heavy rain. From the west bank the track climbs slowly through the forest. About a half hour from the Rivulet there is a good view point of the coast just off the track (817718). Continue on over some hilltops then descend 100m to cross the buttongrass plain of Blowhole Creek. A 250m climb on a tree-root covered track in the forest leads to a campsite on a dry ridge (783722). A 15 minute descent in wet rainforest leads to a small creek (780721) where water is usually found. Climb a further 120m onto the South Cape Range and follow the muddy track to the open Flat Rock Plain. This has excellent views of the coast to the west. Descend steeply west through the mud then forest to enter Granite Beach at its east end beside the waterfall.

Campsites :

- Fletchers Camp (811717). Good shelter, limited space for 2 tents beside the small creek 45 minutes west of South Cape Rivulet.
- Blackhole Plain (801715). Good shelter for several tents on both sides of the plain but no reliable water supply.
- Trackcutters Camp (783722). Large sheltered campsite on the dry ridge 3½ hours from the Rivulet. Water 15 minutes west.
- Granite Beach East (746726). Fair shelter beside the track 200m east of the waterfall. This is the preferred campsite in this bay.

3. Granite Beach — Surprise Bay   3km, 1 to 2 hours

This short section is often combined with the South Cape Range as many parties prefer to camp at Surprise Bay.

From the waterfall at the east end of the bay, traverse the stones and sand of Granite Beach to its western end. This will take 30 to 45 minutes and it is advised to watch out for big waves on the narrow beach. A steep sandy track then rises into the forest followed by a more gradual 160m climb over Shoemaker Point. As you begin descending steeply on the west side a good view of Surprise Bay and the coast is seen. Continue to descend in light forest passing the main camping area to enter Surprise Bay at a short rock face at the east end of the bay.

Campsites :

- Sandstone Creek (743728). Small sites on both banks of this creek in Shoemaker Bay.
- Granite Beach West (735730). Exposed small site beside the most westerly creek.

- Surprise Bay (723740). Sites with good views nearby, beside the main track on the east side of the rivulet. The lagoon water is often brackish. Campfires are allowed at this campsite.
- Surprise Rivulet (722743). Several sites upstream along the east bank close to the lagoon.

4. Surprise Bay — Prion Boat Crossing   9km,3 to 4 hours

After leaving Surprise Bay the well marked track passes through light rainforest then open plains to New River Lagoon.

Leave Surprise Bay at its west end and pass through light rainforest to the open Rocky Plains where good views of the coast are obtained. The staked track crosses the open plains behind Osmiridium Beach then enters a short section of light forest to the top of the dunes overlooking the east end of Prion Beach. Descend to the sand following the steps, do not cause any more erosion by using old unstabilised tracks. *In reverse, from Milford Creek follow the sand south-east to the steps.*

Follow the sand north-west to Milford Creek. At present this is an easy walk across the sand bar. The beach can alter dramatically after heavy storms and sometimes the walk to Milford Creek can require wading along the edge of the permanent dunes. Cross Milford Creek on the sand bar where the creek enters the lagoon. This must be forded and can be a deep wade at high tide or in floods.

Pick up the track on the west bank of Milford Creek and climb steeply up steps onto the top of the lightly timbered sand dunes. The crest is followed west through ti-tree to descend to the campsite near the boat crossing.

Sidetrip : Osmiridium Beach. This is an easy 5 minute walk on a well defined track from Rocky Plains.

Sidetrip : Precipitous Bluff. This towers over New River Lagoon giving tremendous views. It is a long hard climb and should only be attempted by strong, experienced parties. From the boat crossing wade up the lagoon for 3 to 5 hours to camp at the foot of the climbing ridge (659851). The peak can be climbed from this camp in a long return daytrip (p 77).

Campsites :
- Osmiridium Beach. A campsite is found beside Tylers Creek behind the beach (695765). Water from the creek is often of poor quality.
- Eastern Prion (681776). Good campsite on top of the ridge where the track overlooks the east end of the lagoon. Water from an unreliable soak on the lagoon shore.

- Boat Crossing (669793). A large well sheltered campsite on the northern shore. The lagoon water is usually brackish and a 10 minute walk north on the marked track leads to a poor fresh water creek.

5. Prion Boat Crossing — Little Deadmans Bay
9km, 2½ to 3½ hours

Boats are rowed across New River Lagoon. After a long beach walk, light forest and buttongrass are crossed to Little Deadmans Bay at the foot of the Ironbound Range. An easy walk with no climbing.

Cross New River Lagoon using the rowboats. Please ensure that at least one good boat is left on each shore, tied to the provided wire ropes. Oars should be put into the plastic pipes beside the boats. If the oars are missing then spare oars will be found tied to the wire rope post. It is important to tie the boats up properly as in major floods the mooring points are under water. Most parties will take about 1 hour to complete the crossing as three crossings must be done. *(Coming from the west the boats are found beside the lagoon shore where the scrubby sand dune ends.)*

Walk 5km west along the sandy Prion Beach to the other end. This takes 45 to 60 minutes and has good views of the surrounding mountains. Pick up the track at the rocky creek gully at the very west end of the sand. Follow this through forest south-west to Menzies Bluff then west to Turua Beach. There are some fine views along this section.

Enter Turua Beach at its eastern end. Walk west around the small rocky headland in the centre of the bay to the second beach. The track heads inland just before the rocks at the western end of the beach. Follow the forest then buttongrass to the small rocky inlet known as Little Deadmans Bay (593780). Follow the track down to the stony shore and walk along this for 100m to the larger creek and well used campsite. From the west end of Prion Beach to the campsite takes 1½ to 2 hours.

The name of Deadmans Bay has confused walkers and map makers for years. The whole bay which includes Turua Beach is known as Deadmans Bay and the tiny cove has never been given an official name. Little Deadmans Bay is the accepted name for the cove with walkers and eventually it is hoped the maps will follow the same convention.

Campsites :
- Western Prion (629808). Camp on the grassy flats at the west end of the sand. Exposed to southerly storms. Water from the gully where the track leaves the beach.
- Turua Beach West (605807). A good camp in the scrub belt on the east side of Deadmans Creek in the western part of the bay.

Prion Beach and the Ironbounds

- Little Deadmans Bay (593799). Good camping beside the larger creek and on the ridge east of the bay. Campfires are allowed here.

6. Little Deadmans Bay — Louisa River 13km,6 to 9 hours

The track now climbs steeply onto the Ironbounds which is very exposed on top. Extremes of weather occur here. Even in summer there are snowstorms so all parties should be prepared to wait (usually only 1 or 2 days) for the weather to improve and carry full wet weather gear. The track up the Ironbounds from the south side is in forest and usually muddy. The descent on the north side is on a clear rocky ridge. Camping on the range is discouraged and you should start early in the day..

The track leaves Little Deadmans Bay at the larger creek in the bay. It then crosses a small plain and sidles onto a large spur where there is a view of Lousy Bay then continues climbing in very wet and muddy rainforest to the top of the range. The trees are now left and the track follows the exposed crest of the range west for 3 km. There has been a lot of work done here and long sections of boarded track are easily followed. A steep, stony descent then leads to the Louisa River. *(Coming up from Louisa River will take 3 to 4 hours to climb 900m to the crest of the range.)*

Near the Louisa River the track heads north into a large patch of rainforest. There are sheltered campsites on both sides of the river crossing (522848). It is advisable to cross this river before camping as

49

it is prone to flash flooding – all parties should be prepared to wait for the river to subside. The river must be waded and a fixed rope is provided. It is safest to wade on the downstream side of the rope.

Sidetrip : Ironbounds summit. In fine weather a 2 hour sidetrip east along the top of the Ironbounds to the summit gives excellent views.

Campsites :
* Ironbounds Low Camp (570805). Good camp in forest 5 minutes past the creek crossing. This is about 1½ to 2 hours from Deadmans Bay.
* Ironbounds High Camp (570827). A very poor camp on top of the range. Emergency use only as it's very muddy, water is unreliable.
* Louisa River (522848). Excellent sheltered camps in forest on both banks of the river near the crossing. Be careful selecting tent sites after heavy rains as the camping areas occasionally become flooded.

7. Louisa River — Freney Lagoon   17km, 5 to 7 hours

This section crosses flat, open plains. This was once a very muddy track but board walks have improved conditions and you can see what some of the park entry fees have been spent on.

From Louisa River follow the boarded track westwards along the north bank of the river to Louisa Creek. This is crossed on logs to a campsite. Continue to follow the track west over Faraway Creek then climb gradually over the Red Point Hills and descend towards Cox Bight to enter the beach just east of Buoy Creek. (*In reverse the track is found where Buoy Creek meets the beach.*) Continue walking along the sand for a ½ hour past a rocky bluff to Point Eric in the middle of the Cox Bight Bay.

Follow the marked track leading out of the most western camp on the Cox Bight east beach. This leads over to the east end of the west beach. Follow the stony then sandy beach to the outlet of Freney Lagoon (372842).

Sidetrip : Louisa Bay. A beautiful bay which the track misses. The best approach is from Louisa Creek. Leave the South Coast Track about 1km east of Louisa Creek and follow an unmarked track across the buttongrass plains south. Follow the plain to its south-east corner then head down steeply on a rough track through light scrub directly to the beach. This takes about 1 to 1½ hours from the track. A campsite will be found behind the north-west end of the beach, water is from an unreliable soak. At low tide it is sometimes possible to wade out to Louisa Island.

Campsites :

- Louisa Creek. A sheltered campsite on the west bank at crossing.
- Faraway Creek. About 10 minutes west from Louisa Creek.
- Point Eric. Several campsites found along the beach east from Point Eric with the best shelter closest to the point. Water at Goring Creek 5 minutes to the east. An old hut near the creek provides no shelter.
- Freney Lagoon (372842). Good sheltered sites are cut into the scrub belt on both sides of the creek. Good water from the lagoon outlet.

8. Freney Lagoon — Melaleuca
map p 80, 12km, 2½ to 4 hours

An easy walk following a re-aligned track across the buttongrass plains. While longer than the original track there is less mud and overall it is faster. Melaleuca is the site of some small tin mines and has an airstrip and two comfortable huts for bushwalkers.

Walk west along the west beach of Cox Bight to the rocks at end of the sand. Use the steps to leave the beach and the track then heads north-west following the base of the New Harbour Range for 4 km. The track then heads north crossing the marshy valley and follows the original track past Half Woody Hill towards Melaleuca. Approaching Melaleuca a log bridge crosses Moth Creek (323915) and the track leads into the mine workings. Pass the tin shed, turn sharp right onto the vehicle track and follow this to the airstrip. Halfway down the strip on the right a signposted track leads to the Charles King memorial hut. This hut and its newer neighbour are open for walkers to use. All other buildings and the mining machinery in the area are private property. *(When walking south from the huts walk via the airstrip and follow the track from the southern end of the airstrip. At the start of the mine workings turn left circling around an old tin hut to cross Moth Creek on the log bridge. The staked track is then easily followed south-east to Cox Bight.)*

Sidetrips : Several interesting day walks to Mt Melaleuca, Pandora Hill, Hidden Valley, Mt Counsel and the waterfalls are rewarding for those who wish to explore. Most of the area is covered with light scrub and is at times very steep. Walkers are requested to fan-out when visiting these areas to prevent tracks forming.

Campsites :

- In an emergency, rough camping is possible on the plains.
- Melaleuca (322922). Two comfortable huts are open for use with excellent sheltered camping in the nearby forest. Please use the toilet in

Walkers hut at Melaleuca in the 1980's

the forest close to the hut. Do not camp near the houses or in the mine area.

Melaleuca. The mine workings and associated equipment, the rangers hut, the houses and the surrounding garden are all private property and should be treated as such. Denis King built the two huts for walkers use as a memorial to his father, Charles King.

About 50m east of the airstrip, is a large bird hide. This is a substantial building and provides an excellent platform where you can the rare Orange Bellied Parrot. Apart from the two houses, the other large building is the locked rangers hut and boathouse on the edge of the lagoon east of the walkers huts.

Airstrip. Light planes can land on the airstrip at Melaleuca. Food can be flown into here and walkers can fly in or out (p 27).

Route Linking : From Melaleuca the usual continuation is the Port Davey Track (p 64). Also there is some excellent walking around the South West Cape area (p 78).

HUON AND ARTHUR PLAINS TRACKS

This is an all weather track into the South-West. It leads from the Picton River west of Geeveston along the Huon River to Cracroft Crossing. The Arthur Plains are then crossed to meet the Port Davey Track at Junction Creek. It forms a handy access track to the Pictons, Federation Peak (p 146) and the Western Arthurs (p 139).

Maps.   TASMAP 1:100,000 Huon, Old River.
TASMAP 1:25,000 Picton.

Standard. A well formed easy to follow track.

Notes.
- It can be difficult to cross some of the creeks when they are flooded. It is advisable to camp and wait for water levels to drop.
- New roads are being pushed up the Huon River. These are nearing Blakes Opening and may replace the first section of the Huon Track.
- Carry a fuel stove, past Blakes Opening it is a 'Fuel Stove Only' area.

Walking Times. See p 34 for an explanation of the section times - remember to add extra time for stops.
(a) Picton River to Junction Creek will take two long or three medium days to walk.
(b) Cracroft Crossing is a days walk from both ends of the track.
(c) Blakes Opening makes a pleasant return daywalk.

Access. (a) **Picton River (east end).** From Geeveston follow the Arve Road (mainly gravel) for 28km to a road junction 2km before the Tahune Picnic shelter. Turn left onto Picton Road and after a further 1km turn right onto the road signposted 'Huon Track Access'. This crosses the Picton River on a large concrete bridge - park on the left before the bridge. If the gate is closed then you will have to start the walk here.

The only access is by private car or a chartered bus. For a charter contact TWT (p 26). An alternative is to use the daily bus service from Hobart to Geeveston then hire a taxi from there.

(b) **Junction Creek (west end).** This is approached by a half day walk from Scotts Peak Dam along the Port Davey Track (p 58). Some parties continue along the Port Davey Track to Melaleuca.

1. Picton River — Blakes Opening   9km, 1½ to 2½ hours

This follows a bulldozed track providing easy level walking. New forestry roads are being pushed up the Huon River. Some local walkers with keys to the gate, are using Riveaux Road for access by driving to the end and following taped routes downhill to meet the Huon Track before Blakes Opening.

From the bridge over the Picton River, follow Riveaux Road for 1km, turn right and 800m leads to the signposted start of the track where there is a small parking area. Follow the signposted track north for 10 minutes to a track junction and a registration shelter. After signing the book turn left (west). *(From the other direction turn right at the track junction, the left track leads into a quarry. If you miss the junction, cross the quarry and follow the main road out to meet the track at the other end.)* The track was once a road but is now becoming a pleasant walking track. Follow it west for 8km to the shelter hut at Blakes Opening with occasional views of the Huon River.

Sidetrip: Mt Picton A poorly defined pad crosses Blakes Opening and then climbs through forest and scrub to North Lake. The route to North Lake is a days walk each way and the route is only suitable for experienced walkers as the route is scrubby and hard to follow.

Campsites :
- Track Start. There is a reasonable campsite behind the registration shelter at the track junction 10 minutes from the road.
- Blakes Opening Shelter (690278). The three sided hut is in poor condition and is situated beside the track on the east side of the buttongrass clearing. Good camping near the hut. Water from the river. Campfires are allowed here.

2. Blakes Opening — Cracroft Crossing
17km, 5 to 7 hours

The next 17km is a soul destroying switchback track aptly nicknamed the Yo-Yo Track. It is well defined and easy to follow.

Follow the track west across the clearing of Blakes Opening. The track then enters scrubby forest and follows the valley of the Huon River. It climbs and descends steeply over several high ridges to the Cracroft River (573222). Cross the river to the west bank by fording the river at the track crossing. There is no bridge and the crossing can be difficult at high water levels. Follow the track for 10 minutes to the camping area on the edge of the buttongrass plain. This is the site of an old hut. *From the other direction do not cross the river near the camping area, instead follow the old bulldozed track to the river*

From Cracroft Crossing the Eastern Arthur Traverse to Federation Peak (p 146) and the eastern end of the Western Arthurs (p 139) can be directly approached.

Campsites :

- Harrisons Creek (635273). About 2 to 3 hours from Blakes Opening. Reasonable camping in forest near the creek.
- Green Plate Corner (621266). Small camp at the first creek about 1 hour past Harrisons Creek.
- Cracroft Crossing East (574222). Good camping beside the track on the east bank.
- Cracroft Crossing West (573221). Sheltered camping on the edge of the buttongrass plain. Water from the river 80m east.

3. Cracroft Crossing — Junction Creek 19km, 5 to 7 hours

A well staked track along the flat buttongrass plains makes fast, easy walking. This track along the Arthur Plains is also known as McKays Track.

From the camping area (573221) follow the track west for 30m out onto the open buttongrass plain. Follow the track leading west. (The track leading south-west goes to Federation Peak.) This is followed over the low hill line called the Razorback and then further west along the open Arthur Plains to Seven Mile Creek. Cross the first tributary, turn sharp right (the track ahead leads to Moraine K on the Western Arthurs, (p 136) and cross Seven Mile Creek to the campsite area. The Old River map shows the track incorrectly in this area. Continue to follow the main track west to the signposted track junction (411276) near Junction Creek.

Sidetrips : From the Arthur Plains several short trips into the Western Arthurs are possible. This range is very exposed hence all parties must be prepared for extremes of weather. For sidetrips from Junction Creek (p 58).

Sidetrip : Lake Rosanne. Follow the route from Cracroft Crossing to the lake (p 139).

Sidetrip : Mt Scorpio. A return day trip fom Seven Mile Creek on the Arthur Plains. The range is climbed via Moraine K which provides open walking (p 136).

Sidetrip : West Portal to Mt Scorpio. A three day trip which does not require the commitment of the full traverse of the range. From Crac-

Western Arthurs from The Razorback

roft Crossing, climb to Lake Rosanne and camp there. If the weather is fine, the next day is spent going over West Portal and The Phoenix to Promontory Lake or Lake Vesta to camp. An easy half day then leads down Moraine K to Seven Mile Creek (p 139).

Campsites :
- Seven Mile creek (503248). A well sheltered small camp on the east and west side of the double creek crossing. The sites on the west side are prone to flooding.
- Wullyawa Creek (457260). Rough sheltered campsites on the south bank, not recommended.
- Two Mile Creek (441270). A large sheltered camp on the west bank.
- Junction Creek. Many sites, see Port Davey Track (p 59) for details.

Route Linking : From Junction Creek the Port Davey Track (p 58) can be followed north for half a day to Scotts Peak Dam or south for 3 to 4 days to Melaleuca.

PORT DAVEY TRACK

This easy well graded track leads from Scotts Peak Dam, south to Melaleuca at Port Davey. The original Port Davey Track was cut by E.A.Marsden in 1898 as an escape route for shipwrecked sailors. This led from Maydena to Joe Page Bay. The current route follows the old well benched track from Scotts Peak to Spring River and a new track is followed from there to Melaleuca. The old section of track from Maydena to Scotts Peak Dam is impossible to follow as it is either overgrown or flooded by the Pedder Dam.

The track passes right through the South-West but is not as interesting as other major walks in the area. Usually most parties combine this track with the South Coast Track and this is combination is erroneously referred to by some as the South West Track. The first section from Scotts Peak to Junction Creek forms a handy access to the Western Arthurs and the Arthur Plains Track.

Maps.   TASMAP 1:100,000 South Coast Walks or Old River
The track is clearly marked on the maps. The South Coast Walks map is recommended, the Old River map has many errors.

Standard. This is a well graded track which is easy to follow. Most walkers can expect wet feet as it is usually fairly muddy and it passes through a lot of scrub. It should not be underestimated as it is 63km from Scotts Peak Dam to Melaleuca. Some previous hiking experience is desirable. All parties must be self sufficient. See p 34 for an explanation of the section times - remember to add time for stops.

Notes.
- The track crosses no high ranges, but is exposed around the Lost World Plateau.
- Spring and Crossing Rivers flood easily, even in summer. All parties should be prepared to wait until water levels drop.
- After heavy rainfall some of the regular campsites become flooded requiring camp to be pitched on rough locations on higher ground.
- Two row boats are provided for crossing Bathurst Narrows. Please leave one on each side. At times the Narrows cannot be crossed due to rough weather or strong currents and parties may need to wait for more suitable tide and wind conditions.
- As the track follows buttongrass plains it can become very wet and muddy after rainfall.

- The track is generally marked by stakes.
- Many of the campsites are of poor quality and limited in size. The maximum recommended party size is four tents.
- This is a 'Fuel Stove Only' area – no campfires are allowed.

Walking Times. (a) Scotts Peak Dam to Melaleuca takes 3 to 5 days depending on the aspirations of the party.

(b) Scotts Peak to Junction Creek is an easy half day when used as an access to the Western Arthurs or Federation Peak.

Access. (a) **Scotts Peak (north end).** From Hobart follow the Strathgordon Road past Maydena for 31km to Frodshams Pass. Turn left onto the Scotts Peak Road and follow this for a further 33km to Scotts Peak Dam. Turn left towards the Huon River Camping Area and after 500m turn right to the parking area at the start of the track. During the summer months TWT run a regular minibus service (p 26). Light aircraft can also land at the airstrip near Edgar Dam, about 6km east of the track start.

(b) **Melaleuca (south end).** This is in the middle of the South-West. It can be reached by light planes (p 27), boat or the South Coast Track (p 40).

1. Scotts Peak — Junction Creek
map 57, 126, 7km, 2½ to 3½ hours

An easy half day from the road on a well defined track. It undulates over small ridges and creeks to the Arthur Plains. This section of track is gradually improving - much work has been done to the track.

The track heads south-west for 100m to the registration shelter. After filling in the log book follow the well defined foot track south-west through a rain forest then across the plain south of Red Knoll for 2km. At the other end of the plain you will join with the original Port Davey Track which once came from Lake Pedder.

Follow the well defined track south for a further 2 hours, crossing numerous small creeks to a track junction just before Junction Creek. The right track leads to a wading crossing and campsite beside the creek. The left track leads to the cable flood crossing. To prevent spreading a plant disease, wash your boots and gaiters at the creek. The campsite track climbs up to the junction with the Arthur Plains Track (411276) while the cable crossing joins with the Arthur Plains Track 30m east from the junction. (*In reverse the newer cable crossing is found by following the Arthur Plains Track east for 30m to the signposted junction.*) From the junction follow the Port Davey Track south-west for 10 minutes to another camping area tucked in a large copse of

trees (408277). Old map editions show the tracks incorrectly around this area - the South Coast Walks map is correct.

Sidetrips : From Junction Creek there are several short trips up into the Western Arthurs. This range is very exposed. All parties must be well equipped to cope with the extremes of weather.

Sidetrip : Mt Hesperus. A return daytrip from Junction Creek with good views of the southwest from the top. Climb Moraine A to Mt Hesperus and return by the same route (p 118). Water is scarce. This trip could also be done as a 2 day trip camping Lake Cygnus and returning by the same route.

Sidetrip : Mt Hesperus to Mt Orion. A long two day trip camping up in the range. From Junction Creek climb Moraine A to Mt Hesperus and continue on to camp at Square Lake. Return (p 118).

Campsites :
- Huon River Camp (429345). This is at the end of the signposted side road near the dam wall. It is 500m south of the start of the track and has shelter, toilets, and tank water.
- Junction Creek Camp (411278). A good large sheltered campsite beside the creek at the old crossing north of the track junction and a smaller site in the copse of trees beside the track junction.
- Junction Creek Copse (408277). Sheltered camping in the trees at the old hut site and also in the next copse of trees 50m south. Water obtained from the creek to the west.

•

2. Junction Creek — Crossing River
map 146, 10km, 3 to 4 hours

The well defined track crosses open country, skirting around the end of the Western Arthur Range to the Crossing River.

From Junction Creek Copse (408277) follow the track north-west 100m to cross the creek. Here it swings left and crosses the plains westwards for 40 minutes to the Moraine A track junction. (The left track leads to Mt Hesperus.) Take the right track which follows the valley and climbs over the broad saddle north of the Western Arthurs. Descend gradually over many small creeks to the Crossing River. The river is deepest near the eastern bank – be careful wading across as the crossing looks easy but it is often fast flowing

Campsites :

- Moraine A Camp (386267). About 40 minutes west from the shelter hut is where the Moraine A track leaves the Port Davey Track. An exposed wet campsite is found 300m along the Moraine A track at the foot of the ridge. Not recommended.
- Crossing River (324271). Excellent sheltered camping on both banks. Advisable to cross if possible to the opposite bank in case the river floods overnight.

3. Crossing River — Watershed Camp   10km, 3 to 4 hours

Open walking following a staked track leading across the buttongrass covered Crossing Plains to the Spring River valley.

At Crossing River the track will be found 20m north of the crossing on the west bank. Follow the track south-west over several small creeks on the scrubby Crossing Plains past Mt Robinson. The open exposed Spring River-Crossing River watershed is followed for 2km followed by a gradual descent along open ridges. This leads to light scrub then to the first major creek (261207) flowing into the Spring River.

Campsites :

- Copse Shelter (273226). After crossing the watershed the track sidles some hills and passes this sheltered, but poor, sloping camp in a copse of trees. Emergency only.
- Watershed Camp (261207). The first major creek crossed that flows into Spring River. From the old muddy campsite, follow a side track west for 100m into the forest. Dry tent sites with shelter and good water.

4. Watershed Camp — Spring River
14km, 4 to 6 hours

A very well benched track sidles the hills high above the Spring River, crosses the Lost World Plateau then descends and follows the plains beside the river..

Follow the clearly defined track south-west as it sidles the hills above Spring River. There are good views along this section. After 6km the track swings south to cross a creek onto the exposed Lost World Plateau.

Follow the stakes south for 3km across the light scrub of the Lost World Plateau. The track descends from the plateau via a boarded track down a creek gully then crosses a small plain with three creeks. Continue to follow the benched track south sidling the slopes west of Spring River to a track junction (233102). This is 7km south of the Lost

World Plateau. The old and very overgrown Port Davey Track continues south from here for another 6km to Joe Page Bay.

Turn east from the track junction and descend to the bank of Spring River, 5 minutes away. The track reaches the river, crosses on a new log crossing, then follows the east bank downstream 150m to the main campsite. The log crossing can be dangerous in flood if under water.

Campsites :

- Lost World One (213176). Fair shelter beside the first big creek crossed on the plateau, limited sites for 3 tents.
- Lost World Two (212166). A further 15 minutes from the above campsite. Only 2 tentsites.
- Spring Plain Camp (218137). Just south of the Lost World Plateau is a plain with three creeks. A reasonable campsite is found beside the second creek.
- Spring River North (232107). Beside the small creek 15 minutes north of the Spring River crossing. A good, sheltered camp.
- Spring River (235102). A good sheltered camp 150m downstream of the log crossing on the east bank. Prone to flooding. An alternative is to follow the track 500m further and camp at the flood free sites on the open buttongrass plain north of the next creek.

5. Spring River — Bathurst Narrows   10km, 4 to 5 hours

This newer section of track is more undulating than the original Port Davey Track. It crosses ridge tops instead of sidling and most parties find the walking slower because of the climbing required. It crosses open country with great views of the Port Davey area.

Follow the track east out of the campsite (235102) at Spring River onto the buttongrass plain, the track swings north-east for 400m then turns south to cross the next creek (238105). *In reverse, after crossing the creek, follow the track which swings left (west), the track directly ahead to the north is a false lead.* From the creek climb onto the northern end of the ridge leading to Border Hill. Follow this ridge south past Border Hill then descend through a small forest to a large creek (248086). Follow the ridges south a further 2km then descend (passing Forest Camp) into a large scrubby creek (248070). Climb steeply out of this and follow the open ridge tops south with good views of Manwoneer Inlet.

From the best viewpoint, the track heads south-east crossing a small creek. More undulations lead south along the ridge passing Lindsay Hill on the east side, then a gradual descent to Farrell Point with good views of the Bathurst Narrows. A track junction will be reached (255011) just before Farrell Point. The right hand track leads to the camping area in the trees (255010), the left track to the boat crossing, on the eastern side of the point.

If weather conditions are reasonable and you have time then it is advised to do the boat crossing, allow an extra hour for this.

Campsites :

- Forest Camp (250074). Dry sites beside the track in forest. Water from the large creek 5 minutes to the south.
- Manwoneer View (247051). Rough small camp beside the small creek 10 minutes south of the excellent view of Manwoneer Inlet from the ridge, 2½ to 3 hours from Spring River.
- Farrell Point Shelter (255010). A good large camp site in the trees on the west side of the point. Unreliable water 30m south at tiny creek.

6. Bathurst Narrows — Melaleuca   12km, 4 to 5½ hours

After crossing Bathurst Narrows by row boat the track crosses open buttongrass country with extensive views.

Manwoneer Inlet

Cross the Narrows by row boat. Please leave one boat on each side tied up under the trees and turned upside down. It requires three crossings to do this. Two fibreglass dinghies are provided for the crossing. The northern boat is kept at a small sandy cove on the eastern side of Farrell Point. The southern boat is found on the tip of Joan Point. Note that the crossing can be dangerous due to swiftly flowing tides and rough weather and is sometimes too hazardous to attempt. The crossing usually takes 1 hour.

Follow the track south from Joan Point and sidle the hills west of Mt Beattie with good views. Descend to the plains east of Horseshoe Inlet and follow the open plains south to the Melaleuca area. Nearing Melaleuca a vehicle track will be reached. This leads to a bridge over Melaleuca Creek (312919). A further 15 minutes east, following the old vehicle track, leads through some old mine workings to the north-west end of the airstrip. Halfway down the airstrip a track on the left shows the way to the walkers huts.

Sidetrip : Mt Beattie. An easy sidetrip off the track giving good views of Bathurst Harbour. Leave the track 3km south of Joan Point and follow the open ridges east to the top. This has no track and walkers are requested to fan out to prevent track formation. About 2 to 3 hours return to the track.

Campsites :
- Joan Point (285007). This camp is useful when travelling north when the Narrows are too dangerous to cross. Good shelter but little water. Semi-permanent water found 15 minutes south along the track on the lower slopes of Mt Beattie.
- In an emergency, rough camping is possible on the plains from Mt Beattie and Melaleuca.
- Melaleuca (322922). Two huts are provided for walkers use beside the forest near the lagoon. Sheltered camping is also found in the forest near the huts. Please note that all other buildings are private property and not to be used. See the South Coast Track notes (p 53) for further details about Melaleuca.

Route Linking : From Melaleuca the usual continuation is the South Coast Track (p 40). South West Cape (p 78) or exit by light aircraft (p 27) are the other usual options.

PRECIPITIOUS BLUFF

Known to generations of bushwalkers as PB, this mighty mountain rises out of the sea to tower over New River Lagoon on the south coast. It can be climbed from the coast as a two to three day sidetrip but the best way to visit PB is the high level traverse across the Southern Ranges from Lune River. This involves some scrub bashing and is recommended as a classic South-West walk for strong parties. The trip is very varied, crossing open high country, thick scrub, wading New River Lagoon and then onto the surf beaches and variety of the South Coast Track to either Melaleuca or Cockle Creek.

Maps. TASMAP 1:100,000 Huon, South East Cape
TASMAP 1:25,000 Leprena, Precipitious
The new 1:25,000's are highly recommended for this walk as they show the approximate route. Extra maps for the South Coast Track will be also be needed (p 40).

Standard. A rough track through open exposed moors and ridges can be followed to Pindars Peak. From there to Precipitous Bluff the route crosses exposed, scrubby country with intermittent tracks. Because of the conditions this traverse of the Southern Ranges is recommended only to strong, well equipped parties.

Notes.
- The Southern Ranges are very exposed. The weather can be extreme with snowfalls and strong winds in summer. All parties should be well prepared for cold, wet conditions and be prepared to wait for the weather to improve.
- Fuel stoves are essential as this is a 'Fuel Stove Only' area.
- Several of the campsites have only limited shelter so the party size should be limited to 3 tents.
- In dry weather water supplies at many of the campsites are unreliable.

Walking Times. See p 34 for an explanation of the section times - remember to include time for stops.
(a) Lune River to Prion Beach. Parties should allow 6 to 8 days to reach the beach. From there continue along the South Coast Track to Melaleuca or Cockle Creek and this will require another two to three days.

Moores Bridge

(b) Lune River to Pindars Peak and return. Easy walking along the high ridges making a pleasant 3 to 4 day walk in fine weather.

(c) Precipitous Bluff from New River Lagoon. With the long wade up the lagoon, parties will need to allow 2 to 3 days to climb the mountain as a side trip from the South Coast Track.

Access. (a) **Lune River (east end).** This small town is 105km south of Hobart on the Huon Highway. Follow the road south from Lune River for 2km to Ida Bay. Turn right onto South Lune Road 300m south of the railway crossing. Follow this road for 5km to an open valley and road junction (887884). Turn left and the road leads uphill towards the old quarry, leave cars well off the road. The start of the track is opposite the car park and is signposted. Sign the book at the information shelter before starting.

During the summer months access is obtained using the regular bus service to Cockle Creek. Booking should be made with the bus service (p 26) as the track is off the main road. If walking out without a booking then follow the roads out to Ida Bay from where the bus can be caught at its scheduled times.

(b) **Prion Beach (west end).** This beach is approached from either the west or east by the South Coast Track (p 40). This takes 2 to 3 days from either direction. It can also be approached by boat.

1. Lune River — Moonlight Creek   8km, 4 to 5 hours

This section follows a well cut track that climbs through the forest on Marble Hill then leads to an exposed walk over the scrubby Moonlight Flats. The track is easy to follow.

Start at the track (886876) 60 metres before the quarry. (It will take an extra 1 hour to walk from Ida Bay to the quarry for those without transport.) Follow the muddy track west for 20 minutes to a camp beside Mystery Creek. A further 5 minutes along the old railway formation leads to an abandoned quarry (874876). Pick up the track on the right side (north) of the quarry. This climbs south along the lip of the quarry then heads south-west into the forest. The main track climbs steadily passing some minor sidetracks which lead to caves.

A steady 2 hour climb in the forest leads to a small campsite on the edge of Moonlight Flats (859876). A further one hour uphill through the ti-tree leads to some small tarns on the scrubby tops. Follow the foot pad west for about 45 minutes to Moonlight Creek (829874). *(Coming east from the campsite follow the foot pad due east (magnetic) across the highest part of Moonlight Flats.)*

Campsites :
- Mystery Creek (875879). Well sheltered camp only 20 minutes from the start of the track.
- Moonlight Flats (859876). There is reasonable shelter for two tents on the east edge of the flats but no permanent water.
- Moonlight Creek (829874). Good shelter for 2 tents hidden in trees near the top of the creek. Water from the small creek.

2. Moonlight Creek — Pigsty Ponds   6km, 2½ to 3½ hours

This section gives easy walking over very exposed open country with rough unmarked tracks to follow.

From Moonlight Creek (829874) cross the scrubby Moonlight Flats westwards directly towards Hill One (816874). Climb this hill through the big break in the scarpline onto the open tops above. In fine weather the first views from here of Federation Peak and PB are magnificient. Follow the occasional cairns over open grass west down to the saddle (808873). At the start of the scrub follow the rough, muddy track which sidles the northern slopes of Hill Two (Table Top ridge) to the south-east end of Moores Bridge. Sidle Hill Three (795861) on its north-west side then follow the ridge south-west over the rocky top of Hill Four (789857). Continue south-west down the ridge over a small knoll then down to Pigsty Ponds.

Sidetrip : The Hippo. Easily approached along the ridge from Hill Three. Fan-out on the ridge. Allow about 3 hours return.

Sidetrip : Reservoir Lakes. A well defined track exists between Reservoir Lakes and Pigsty Ponds. Tracks exist along both banks of the upper Reservoir Lake, the eastern side is easier to walk with packs. It takes about 20 minutes with packs from Reservoir Lakes to Pigsty Ponds.

Sidetrip : Arndell Falls (792843). From Pigsty Ponds walk south to the head of the D'Entrecasteaux River then head down the un-tracked northern bank to the falls. You are requested to fan-out to prevent tracks forming. Reasonable views from the cliff top to the north.

Campsites :
- Hill One Saddle (808873). A very exposed site in the saddle between Hill One and Two. Water from the tarns to the east on Hill One. There is another similar exposed camp between Hills Two and Three.
- Pigsty Ponds (779847). Two semi sheltered tent sites exist beside the outlet creek of the highest lake. More exposed sites are located on the opposite shore of the lake and around the other major lake.
- Reservoir Lakes (781853). Several campsites with good shelter cut into the scrub on both sides of the creek joining the two lakes. This site is preferable to Pigsty Ponds in poor weather.

3. Pigsty Ponds — Ooze Lake   4km, 2 to 3 hours

Although this section is very short, most parties make it a full day by visiting Mt La Perouse as a side trip. This is recommended if the weather is suitable. The main route follows open exposed tops, then a cut track through scrub to Ooze Lake.

If at Reservoir Lakes walk up to Pigsty Ponds, a 15 minute walk. From Pigsty Ponds, walk south descending a little then follow a winding track, following cairns up the rocky hill between Mt La Perouse and Maxwell Ridge. A large stone arrow on the ground (780841) will be seen on the ascent and this points left to the track leading to Mt La Perouse. Continue south-west from the arrow into a light scrubby saddle (779838) then climb steeply west up open slopes onto Maxwell Ridge. Follow the narrow ridge north to where it widens to a plateau. Pick up the cairns on the western edge (772841) marking the track and follow this down south-east through scrub into King Billy Saddle. A rough cut track then sidles through the scoparia covered northern slopes of Knife Mt to some small valleys that lead into Ooze Lake at the outlet creek (758834).

Sidetrip : Mt La Perouse. Leave the main route at the stone arrow marked on the ground (780841). Sidle south-east into the saddle then follow the open ridge south-east to the rocky plateau of Mt La Perouse. This takes about 1½ to 2 hours return from the stone arrow (2 to 3 hours return from Pigsty Ponds).

Sidetrip : Knife Mountain and Lake Mountain circuit. The circuit around Ooze Lake has views and plenty of mild scrub, 2 to 3 hours.

Campsites :
- Ooze Lake (758833). Passable sites on the eastern shore and more exposed sites near the outlet.

4. Ooze Lake — Leaning Teatree Saddle
6km, 4 to 5 hours

Open walking leads over Pindars Peak to Pandanni Knob. From here thick scrub is encountered and progress becomes slower to Leaning Teatree Saddle. In fine weather the views are grea;, in mist, navigation can be awkward.

Follow the open north shore of Ooze Lake then climb south-west up the open slopes of Lake Mt following occasional cairns. Cross the western flanks of Lake Mt to the saddle before Pindars Peak (753828). Here the route becomes well defined again and a cairned track climbs south-west up the ridge past a prominent rock knob. The track crosses to the south-east side of the ridge and climbs the terraced slopes to regain the ridge crest just north-east of the summit of Pindars Peak. Drop packs here and scramble steeply towards the summit. A final short rocky climb leads to the summit area. In fine weather the views of the coast and the Southern Ranges are excellent.

Return to the packs and immediately descend the short gully on the north side of the ridge until you can traverse west keeping up high close to the cliffs. This leads onto the main ridge just past the summit rocks. Walk along the open ridge north-west following a roughly cairned track. This passes through light scrub down to Pandanni Knob (735826). From here the ridge becomes very scrubby. From Pandanni Knob follow very rough tracks north-west down the ridge through thick, high scrub to a broad saddle known as Pandanni Saddle. Cross the saddle to its northern side where there are some pools and a reasonable campsite (728835). *(Going towards Pindars Peak the rough track should be found as the scrub is very thick.)* Follow more rough tracks in the heavy scrub north-west over the next hilltop and

Approaching Pindars Peak

down to the open clearing at Leaning Teatree Saddle (724838) – about 45 minutes from the previous campsite.

Campsites :
- Pindars Ridge. Small campsite for 2 or 3 tents in a small valley on the ridge top 600m north-west of Pindars Peak. No close water supply except in wet conditions.
- Pandanni Knob (735826). Exposed camping with light shelter from bushes. Water very unreliable.
- Pandanni Saddle (728835). In the saddle north from Pandanni Knob there is a campsite with reasonable shelter, water from semi-permanent pools.
- Leaning Teatree Saddle (724838). Some fair tentsites cut into the scrub with minimal shelter. Water from semi-permanent pools.

5. Leaning Teatree Saddle — Wylly Plateau
3km, 2 to 2½ hours

More scrub bashing along the high ridges to the plateau. Ooze Lake to Wylly Plateau can be walked in one day. In dry conditions water can be a problem along this section and another alternative is to walk from Leaning Tea Tree Saddle to P.B. Low Camp in one day.

From Leaning Teatree Saddle follow rough tracks north-west through the thick scrub to the top of the next hill. The scrub now eases to waist deep as you descend down into the next saddle where there is another possible campsite (719844) about 1 hour from Leaning Tea-tree Saddle. Climb north through light scrub onto a long ridge and follow the semi-open ridge north to Mt Wylly. Climb 100m up the south-west slope of Mt Wylly until it is possible to traverse north at the rock bands to the north-west ridge of Mt Wylly. (It is easy to climb to the summit via this ridge.) Follow this ridge down onto Wylly Plateau. This is covered in low vegetation. *In reverse, from the plateau climb up to the first scarp line then traverse right.* Follow the south edge of the plateau to the west where the main campsite will be found (714680).

Sidetrip : Mt Wylly. Best climbed via the rocky north-west ridge. About a half hour return to the main route.

Sidetrip : Mt Victoria Cross. About 2 to 3 hours return from the campsite. Follow Wylly Plateau north to the peak. Avoid the first rocky summit by following the wide gully on the east.

Campsites :
    Windy Saddle (719844). Very exposed camping at the saddle 1 hour north from Leaning Teatree Saddle, water from unreliable pools.
    Wylly Plateau (714680). A camp with poor shelter almost on the highest part of the plateau. Water is sometimes difficult to find here and comes from unreliable pools or the creek to the east.

6. Wylly Plateau — Low Camp   5km, 5 to 6 hours

This involves more scrub bashing then a rough, rocky, moraine ridge to the foot of Precipitous Bluff. If time and weather permits it is worthwhile to continue up to Plateau Camp.

From the western end of Wylly Plateau follow rough tracks through waist deep scrub down the ridge and up onto the next hill to the north-west (705864). A poor dry campsite will be found on top about 1 hour from Wylly Plateau. The broad scrubby saddle to the north must now be crossed. This is very scrubby and is thickest on the north side of the saddle where it becomes low forest. Follow rough pads down towards the saddle. Conditions regularly change here, often you can follow a very rough track the whole way across but if the markers have been removed then you will have to find your own route. Avoid descending into the valleys below the saddle – eventually climb north-west up to the obvious saddle (701876) on Kameruka Moraine.

A rough campsite (Tramp Camp) is found in the saddle and this is about 3½ to 4½ hours from Wylly Plateau. From this camp follow the rough track south-west along the crest of the rocky and scrubby Kameruka Moraine for a further 1½ hours towards Precipitous Bluff. Low Camp will be found 100m north-west of the saddle below Precipitous Bluff.

Campsites :
- Wylly West Hill (705864). On top of the hill 1km west of the Wylly Plateau is a poorly sheltered site, no water.
- Tramp Camp (701876). Reasonable shelter in the saddle on Kameruka Moraine. Water is very unreliable.
- Low Camp (687868). Fair shelter with water from soaks or off the rocks at the foot of PB. In very dry conditions it may be necessary to climb to the waterfall for water.

7. Low Camp — Plateau Camp   1km, 1½ to 2 hours

A steep, rough climb up the improbable looking east face of Precipitous Bluff.

From Low Camp head west following vague tracks through scrub to the foot of the cliffs of Precipitious Bluff. The cliffs above can be climbed in several places. The easiest route to ascend is on the north side of the major creek that flows down the face. This gives access to an open, high valley above and a track is easily followed up the right hand side to Plateau Camp at the top of the valley.

Sidetrip : Precipitious Bluff Summit. From Plateau Camp follow the ridge crest south for 15 to 20 minutes to the summit cairn where a log book is located. The views are excellent in fine weather.

Campsites :
- Plateau Camp (678872). Scattered sites at the top of the valleywith poor shelter. Water from pools or from down the creek just above the waterfall. Select toilet areas outside the water catchment

8. Plateau Camp — New River Lagoon
3½ km, 4 to 6 hours downhill

The track follows the base of the cliffs of Precipitous Bluff then descends steeply to the lagoon. The track is poorly marked and care is needed to follow it on the descent ridge. The 1:25,000 Precipitous map incorrectly shows the route through the cliffs.

Precipitious Bluff

From Plateau Camp locate the cairned route at the top of a gully 100m north of main campsite. Descend west into the gully and about half way down exit left by climbing up some grassy slopes. Traverse south across the slopes and down a rocky ramp into the next gully. An impressive amphitheatre of cliffs tower above.

Descend steeply to the bottom of this gully about 1 to 1½ hours from Plateau Camp. Now follow the base of the cliffs south through high scrub across several gullies for 1 hour to a large pool which is apparently permanent. A further 15 minutes along the cliffs leads to a major gully and 150m beyond this the track turns sharp right onto the descent ridge.

The track follows the crest of the ridge south-west and is reasonably well defined. About half way down the ridge divides and the track follows the more northern branch. Care is required here to locate the correct route as the track wanders through a limestone area. If the track is lost, descend south-west (220 degrees magnetic) to the creek and follow the creeks out to the lagoon. The track leads to a cave at the foot of the spur from which a creek emerges. Follow the meandering creek downstream to New River Lagoon.

Sidetrip : Precipitous Bluff from New River Lagoon. The mountain can be climbed in a very long return daytrip from the lagoon. This should only be attempted by fast, strong parties as several groups have been benighted when attempting this.

(Coming from the lagoon follow the taped cavers track upstream to the cave at the foot of the spur south of Damper Creek. The track climbs steeply up to the right of the cave. Follow the ridge up to the foot of the cliffs. The track turns north following the cliff base to a major gully. A very difficult route does lead up this gully but the preferable route is to continue following the cliff base north. After an hour cross a narrow gully by climbing up into it and down again and shortly after enter the ascent gully. This is easily climbed until it ends then exit left into the next gully which leads to the top.)

Campsites :
- Cliff Bivouac. A small bivouac is located below the track near the foot of the cliffs close to the permanent pool.
- New River Lagoon (658850). A sheltered campsite beside the lagoon on the south bank of Damper Creek. Water from the creek as the lagoon water is often brackish.

9. New River Lagoon — Prion Beach   7km, 3 to 6 hours

From here the best way is to simply wade down the lagoon as it is usually ankle to knee deep. It is handy if one person carries a wading pole as this makes it easier (and drier) to locate hidden logs and to find the sandbar past each creek. Note that if the river is in flood it can become very difficult to wade and the scrubbash along the shore has taken some parties 1½ days.

Wade down the lagoon to the large creek (658811) near the end. This usually cannot be waded past. Go inshore 100m and cross the two tributaries on large logs. Continue wading to the boat crossing on the South Coast Track. *(Coming up the lagoon it is important to locate the campsite (658850). From the lagoon the sandy beaches with some very large gum trees behind are an obvious feature. This can be confirmed by a bearing on the apparent highest point on the Ironbounds, 276 degrees True (263 degrees Magnetic)).*

Campsites:
- Several of the creeks flowing into the lagoon provide sites if needed.
- Prion Beach. See South Coast Track (p 48).

Route Linking : The route is completed by walking along the South Coast Track (p 48), west to Melaleuca or east to Cockle Creek.

SOUTH WEST CAPE

A visit to this rugged cape is recommended to most walking parties. The granite cape juts out for 3km into the wild Southern Ocean to form a spectacular beginning to the South-West. The area has excellent coastal scenery with high headlands towering above small bays and sandy beaches. The most popular walk is from Melaleuca to Ketchem Bay or Wilson Bight and returning the same way.

The walking is fairly easy with rough unmarked tracks crossing fairly open country around the coastline. This area has become very popular and some track work and track re-routing is planned over the next couple of years, so expect changes.

Maps.   TASMAP 1:100,000 Old River, South West Cape, Port Davey
TASMAP 1:100,000 South Coast Walks
TASMAP 1:25,000 Melaleuca, Cox, Telopea
Map 1:50,000 p 91

Standard. The route crosses open untracked country around the coast. It climbs over some exposed high ridges and these can be very unpleasant to cross in wet, windy weather. From Melaleuca to South West Cape is along well defined pads and most walkers will find navigation fairly easy. The remainder of the circuit from Wilson Bight north has sections of untracked country to cross and parties should have navigational experience off marked tracks.

Notes.
- Some of the bays visited have sheltered campsites. To stay more than one night can be rewarding.
- Some extra time should be allowed for the weather and to fully enjoy this coast line.
- This is a 'Fuel Stove Only' area, no campfires are allowed.
- There is very little scrub in this area and as a result there are many route variations. The notes describe the most commonly used routes. If you are crossing untracked country it is suggested you fan-out to prevent tracks from forming.

Walking Times. There are several trips which are considered standard. Other combinations are equally good. All routes start and end at Melaleuca or Cox Bight.

(a) To New Harbour and Ketcham Bay. Return via the same route. For a relaxing trip, 3 to 5 days is suggested.

(b) To the Cape via Ketcham Bay. Return via the same route. A longer but easy walk. Allow 3 to 5 days.

(c) The full circuit. Walk via Ketcham Bay to the Cape then north to Window Pane Bay, Noyhener Beach and east to Melaleuca. Has some long walking days crossing un-tracked country and is the best walk for experienced walkers. Allow 6 to 9 days.

Access. Melaleuca or Cox Bight are the start and finish of any walk to South West Cape. These two places are close together and are approached by The South Coast Track (p 53), The Port Davey Track (p 64), light aircraft (p 27) or by boat.

1A. Melaleuca — New Harbour   11km, 2½ to 3½ hours

An easy half day along the usually wet buttongrass plains. It is possible to walk directly toward New Harbour over the rough buttongrass but navigation is easier if the described route is followed.

From Melaleuca follow the South Coast Track (p 53) south for 5km past Half Woody Hill. The track crosses the valley towards the base of the northern end of the New Harbour Range. Here there is a track junction. Turn right and leave the main track. Follow the foot pad west around the northern end of the New Harbour Range. This is part of the original South Coast Track and is marked by old steel stakes.

The track then heads south along the edge of the New Harbour Range. After passing through a small saddle (327843), the track crosses an open plain. From here there has been several variations over the years. The current track crosses George Creek and follows the buttongrass lead parallel to the lagoon south for about 400m then turns west and follows a track through scrub to a small campsite on the grassy east bank of the lagoon (319829). Walk 150m south to the beach, wade across the creek (this can be deep at high tide) and walk west along the beach to the main camping area above the creek in the centre of the bay. Use the track to enter the campsite to prevent damage to the shoreline scrub which protects the campsites.

1B. Cox Bight — New Harbour (low level)
10km, 2 to 3½ hours

From Cox Bight there are two routes to New Harbour. The low level route is easier and the only route to use when the New Harbour Range is under cloud.

From Freney Lagoon follow the beach west then north-west along the South Coast Track for 4km sidling the base of the New Harbour

New Harbour

Range (p 53) to the track junction at the northern end of the range.Turn left onto the minor track and follow the route described in 1A to New Harbour.

1C. Cox Bight — New Harbour (high level)

8km, 3 to 4 hours

A spectacular route in fine weather with excellent views from the top of the New Harbour Range. The route is difficult with a heavy pack as it climbs very steeply and there are no formed tracks. Do not cross the range in poor visibility.

From Freney Lagoon follow the beach west then the South Coast Track inland to the open plains. From here, climb onto the top of the New Harbour Range. It is best to follow the track inland for 1 km and climb one of the more gentle ridges rather than heading directly up the steep ridge near the beach. Once on top, walk west across the

81

open tops, walkers are requested to fan-out to prevent tracks form-ing. Descend the steep ridge heading south-west then west to the but-tongrass plain behind the east end of the New Harbour beach. You will meet the low level track on the edge of the scrub beside the la-goon. Follow this to the lagoon shore and beach then west along the beach to the main camping area.

Campsites :
- Falls Creek (319829). Small camping area on the east bank of the la-goon 150m behind the beach. Do not camp on the grassy flats as they are tidal. Water from a tiny unreliable creek, the lagoon is brackish.
- New Harbour (309830). Excellent large camping area in open forest above the creek in the centre of the bay. Keep to the access track to protect the sheltering scrub. Water from the creek.

2. New Harbour — Ketchem Bay
5km, 2½ to 3½ hours

An easy half day with some short ridges to climb over with good views of the coastline. Current plans are to re-route parts of this track so expect changes and follow any signs.

Leave New Harbour at the west end of the beach. Currently the track climbs very steeply to the ridge top, heads south 1 km then de-scends steeply to Hidden Bay. It is planned to re-route this over the 1998-99 summer to head around the northern end of the high ridge then sidle the western base of the ridge to Hidden Bay.This will be a much easier route. The track curently enters Hidden Bay at the large sand blow (299811), the new track will probably enter the eastern end of the beach. Due to the steep climb it is 1½ to 2½ hours from New Harbour to Hidden Bay, the new track is expected to take about a ½ hour less to walk.

Leave Hidden Bay at the sand faces at the western end of the beach and follow the track through the narrow scrub belt to the but-tongrass behind. *(From the west the track is located where the scrub belt is thinnest.)* A short 40m climb leads onto the ridge to the west (293807). Walk north along this ridge a ½ km then descend west and cross the creek in the valley where it is scrub free. Walk west over a ridge and a small valley to the larger ridge above Ketchem Bay (286807). It is also proposed to re-route this section so that the track follows the ridge north-west circling around the head of the tiny valley then follows the ridge south to meet the current track on the ridge above Ketchem Bay. This ridge provides excellent views. From the ridge top, descend west to the sand at Ketcham Bay. The last 30m to the beach is down a steep track in thick scrub.

Campsites :

- Hidden Bay (295809). A small campsite on the west bank of the creek in the centre of the bay.
- Ketchem Bay East (281803). Reasonable camping in the forest on both banks of the lagoon of Ketchem Creek. Good swimming in the lagoon. Water from the waterfall at the western end of the bay.
- Ketchem Bay West (279802). A sheltered campsite on the south bank of the small creek at the west end of the bay. Water from the waterfall at the north end of the camping area.

3. Ketchem Bay — Wilson Bight   4km, 2 to 3½ hours

An easy climb leads over the Amy Range with more views from the top.

Start at the most northern track beside the waterfall at the west end of the bay (279802). Follow the rough track uphill through the forest to the buttongrass slopes. *(Coming down, the track is found south of the small tree covered knob 50m above the sand.)* Pass the small knob on its south side and follow the ridge which climbs west to the top of the Amy Range (268799) for excellent views. Walk west along the crest for 500m then follow the undulating open ridge which leads south from the range (264799). Follow this ridge south until it ends then descend steeply west onto the plains behind Wilson Bight.

There are several routes into Wilson Bight. One route heads south and enters the beach via the dry gully 20m west of the creek. From there you can follow the shore around into the next small bay. The other route heads west crossing the plains then rounds the obvious hill (258790) on its north side. Passing the hill, head south then southwest crossing the small gully to the next ridge (256786). Follow the crest of this ridge south and descend the ridge directly to enter a well sheltered campsite. *(When coming from the beach follow the rough track leading up the hill at the back of the campsite.)*

Campsites :

- Wilson Bight (256786). The campsite with the best shelter is located 50m east of the creek with the small waterfall. *(For parties coming from the west this is in the first sandy bay.)* There are several other sites scattered around the bay as well.

4. Sidetrip — South West Cape   9km, 6 to 8 hours

Campsites near the Cape are exposed and most parties visit the Cape as a return daytrip from Wilson Bight. Without full packs, it is much faster to walk out to the cape and most go to the view of the last knoll.

If you want to visit the actual end of the cape then you will need a rope, ascenders and a very early start. Times vary widely for this sidetrip.

From the campsite, follow the beach west, climb over a low headland and cross the next beach. This is the most western bay in Wilson Bight and has a stone beach. Locate the track beside the creek, this heads west. It climbs steeply up the ridge crest through the coastal forest belt to the open spur. *(When coming down, keep to the ridge crest to stay on the track.)* Climb the steep ridge following the well defined pad to the open tops of Mt Karamu. Cross these tops to the first (lower) summit of Mt Karamu (237787). The steep ridge south-west from here leads to the cape. Descend this ridge and then zigzag along the ridge tops out towards the cape until the granite and scrub is reached. Cross the first broad scrubby saddle, if needed a poor campsite will be found down the next gully on the north-west side (221768).

Follow the track along the crest of the ridge through thickening scrub to a really good view (220758) of the last knoll on the cape. This

South West Cape

view point is about 40 minutes from the start of the scrub and is the turning point for most parties. To go to the very end from here will require 15m of rope to descend a rock wall in the next saddle. It will be necessary to abseil and prussick this wall. From the saddle the last knoll is easily climbed. If visiting the end allow lots of time as most parties are very slow at abseiling and ascending the rock wall. Return by the same route.

5. Wilson Bight — Window Pane Bay   15km, 7 to 8 hours

A long day along the exposed tops of the South West Cape Range. Some light scrub is encountered. While a light pad exists along most of the route, navigational skill is required in misty weather as there are no markers on the route. Before leaving Wilson Bight, wash your boots, gaiters and tent pegs. This is necessary to prevent spreading the Root Rot disease to the northern area of this circuit.

From Wilson Bight follow the track towards South West Cape as far as the lower summit of Mt Karamu (237787). Walk north-west over the higher summit (234793) and follow the open ridges north

South West Cape from Window Pane Bay

Island Bay

losing height until you can climb east onto the South West Cape Range (243808). It is also possible to walk directly from Wilson Bight to the South West Cape Range. This route has some mild scrub, is less scenic and is discouraged by management.

Follow the top of the South West Cape Range north. Parties are requested to fan-out along the range to prevent a track forming. Some light scrub leads onto the highest point (229841) of the range. The crest becomes clear again and, heading north, the range descends gently over the next 2km until a steep drop of 150m leads to a plain on the ridge top. Walk 400m north across this undulating plain to meet a staked track crossing from east to west (228866). This is part of the 1966 South Coast Track alignment. The route to the east led into Window Pane Creek and over Mt Melaleuca – it was scrubby and extremely steep. The track markers have been removed from this route and it is now very difficult to follow.

To descend to Window Pane Bay follow the staked track west over the plain then steeply down a ridge to enter the forest behind Window Pane Bay. Follow the track through open forest for 30 to 40 minutes to exit onto the beach 300m south of Window Pane Creek.

Campsites :

- South West Cape Range. In fine weather exposed camping on the top of the range is possible. Water can usually be found in pools just north of the highest point of the range.
- Window Pane Bay (210874). Good campsites with minimal shelter on the north bank of Window Pane Creek. Water from the main creek.

6. Window Pane Bay — Noyhener Beach
map 91, 7km, 3 to 4½ hours

This section continues to follow the coast north to another beautiful beach. A staked track exists providing excellent views and easy walking. The stakes are difficult to follow in places.

Go up the scrubby valley beside the camp at Window Pane Bay Twenty years ago this was an open sand blow and vegetation has consolidated the sand. The marked track will be picked up at the top of this on the left side. Follow this track through light scrub and up onto the open ridge which runs north, parallel to the coast. This track is part of the 1966 South Coast Track alignment. Follow the stakes north along this ridge, sidling the west side of the highest point (202895) then gradually descend across the big open creek valleys behind the coast until almost on the coast at Faults Bay. (Many of the stakes along this section are down) The track follows the plains north for 1km then passes through the coastal scrub belt to the rocky coastline (187923). *(Coming from Noyhener Beach this track can be difficult to locate. A cairn on the rocks marks the start. This is due west (Magnetic) from the north end of Mutton Bird Island and is just past the some awkward rocky coves which are difficult to cross at high tide.)*

Follow the rocky coast north for ½ to 1 hour to the sand. It is best to keep to the rocks if possible because the coastal scrub is very thick and tough. Follow Murgab Creek to where it turns inland into the scrub.

Sidetrip : Stephens Bay and Hilliard Head. A very enjoyable daytrip from Murgab Creek. Follow the sand west to Chatfield Point. Rock hop around this with one short climb over some headlands to Stephens Bay. Follow the beach to the most northern creek (158962) to find a campsite and water 1½ hours from Murgab Creek. The open country to the north is easily crossed to Spain Bay, Going Hill and Hilliard Head. Return along the beaches. It is also possible to follow the sand dunes behind Chatfield Point to Stephens Bay; it is difficult to link the open leads together and you must expect some scrub bashing.

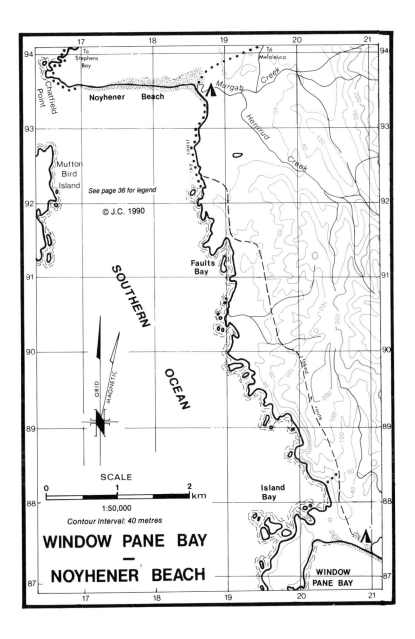

SOUTH WEST CAPE :
WINDOW PANE BAY — NOYHENER BEACH

Campsites :
- Murgab Creek (186936). A large excellent campsite is hidden behind the scrubby sand dune on the south side of the creek. The easiest route to it is to cross the creek 50m below the bend where it swings south as it exits from the dunes. Locate the foot track which heads east across the scrubby dune to the sheltered camp. This is located in tall ti-tree and is close to the creek. You can also approach the camp by a deep wade across the creek where the scrub starts on the north bank.

7. Noyhener Beach — Melaleuca   17km, 8 to 11 hours

A long day over open untracked country. Some light scrub is encountered in places. Times can vary widely as there is no single route, most parties take a long day to get to Melaleuca. There are two basic routes to choose from.

(i) This heads nearly due east to the Port Davey Track and most parties would choose this route. From Murgab Creek climb north onto the top of the sand dunes and descend north-east into light scrub. Cross this and walk east over the open ridges and plains and climb steeply onto the South West Cape Range. Descend to Hannant Creek and cross this where the scrub appears thinnest. Climb the open ridges onto the Pasco Range. From here there are also two main variations. One is to follow the clearly defined ridge to the east of Pasco Creek to Horseshoe Inlet, walk the shores swimming across Horseshoe Creek. The other is to descend steeply east to the plains and head north-east to the south edge of the swamp at Horseshoe Inlet. Follow the edge of the swamp east. This avoids the scrubby creeks further south. Climb over the hills to the east and descend to the Port Davey Track 3km north of Charlies Hill. Follow the Port Davey Track (p 64)south to Melaleuca.

(ii) This is the longer but more scenic route. As for (i) head out onto the ridges and plains behind Noyhener Beach. Follow these plains north for 4km, parallel to Hannant Inlet. Cross the north edge of the South West Cape Range and climb Mt Curran. From here descend east to Horseshoe Inlet and follow the shore to the east end of the bay. Horseshoe Creek is narrow but deep and requires a short swim to cross it.

Note that there are patches of light scrub on all routes. Careful route selection will reduce these to a minimum. Walkers are requested to fan-out in this area to prevent tracks from forming. During dry spells the Horseshoe Inlet swamp is sometimes dry and makes a pleasant alternative route.

Spain Bay & Davey Head

Campsites :
- Poor camping near creeks on the rough buttongrass plains.
- Melalueca (322922). Two comfortable huts with for bushwalkers. See p 53 for further details.

WEST COAST

The coast from Macquarie Harbour to Port Davey provides some magnificient walking along a rugged coastline. Initially it appears as an undisturbed wilderness and really shouldn't appear in a guide. The reality is that while it is rarely visited by bushwalkers it is extensively visited by fishing boats which frequent the west coast and can't be regarded as untouched wilderness. The walking is mainly along the ever present rocks with some relief provided by sandy bays, buttongrass plains and extremely thick scrub. It is an area highly recommended for experienced off-track walking parties.

The coast itself can be divided into three distinct sections according to the access points. The northern section from Cape Sorrell to Hibbs Lagoon provides some easy coastal walking and is highly recommended for first time extended walks. The middle section from Hibbs Lagoon to Low Rocky Point offers very rough walking conditions. Cliffs border the ocean involving lengthy scrambles and extremely thick scrub must be pushed through to bypass impassable coastal sections. For the southern section from Low Rocky Point to Port Davey the terrain relents and provides easy walking across extensive buttongrass plains. To complete the area brief notes are given for linking across to the Port Davey Track.

Maps.   TASMAP 1:100,000 Cape Sorrell, Spero, Olga, Port Davey. TASMAP 1:25,000 Kelly, Table Head, Varna, Hibbs, Endeavor, Montgomery,Mainwaring/Veridian, Lewis

Standard. All parties must be self sufficient and able to cope with emergencies as this is a remote area. There are no tracks and little difficulty with navigation as the coast is followed most of the time. The first section to Hibbs Lagoon is easy and is recommended for all parties for a first visit. The section from Hibbs Lagoon to Low Rocky Point is very difficult in places and is recommended to groups who are experienced with extensive rock hopping and heavy scrub bashing. The third section from Low Rocky to Bond Bay is generally fairly easy and recommended for groups who have some experience at choosing the easiest routes through scrub bands.

Notes.
- The coastline can be a remote place and all parties must be self sufficient and resourceful in an emergency. It may be possible to get assistance from a fishing boat but this cannot be relied upon.

◀ *Coast walking south of Endeavour Bay*

- Rivers along the coast can flood quickly becoming very dangerous to cross. Fortunately they fall quickly as well and it is recommended that parties should wait for flooded streams to drop before crossing.
- The coast itself can be followed except when the seas become huge (above 6 metres). In such conditions it may be advisable to wait a day for the seas to ease rather than spend some of the time in the scrub to avoid the ocean.
- Extra time must be allowed for the conditions above.
- While driftwood is plentiful along the shore it is still necessary to carry a fuel stove for cooking in very wet weather.
- The weather in summer along the coast is mostly fine which is a sharp contrast to the inland ranges. However it is advisable to be equiped as for any other south-west walk as it does occasionally pour down.
- The notes presented here are in a format suitable for experienced walkers to plan a successful trip. They describe only the major obstacles and still leave a lot of route finding around the many gulches and other obstacles. If the notes appear too brief, then choose another walk with more detail and gain experience before venturing along this remote coast.

Walking Times. There are various itineraries from which to choose and the more obvious are suggested here. Expect wide variations from the given times as there is no clearly defined route.

(a) Cape Sorrell to Hibbs Lagoon. This requires 4 to 5 days to walk. Allow at least one extra day for flooded streams. An interesting addition is to include a return visit to Point Hibbs which requires another 2 days.

(b) Hibbs Lagoon to Low Rocky Point then north to Moores Valley or Birches Inlet. With some lee time 15 to 16 days is suggested for this walk. It can be shortened by 1 to 2 days by following the old exploration tracks east from Rhueben or Sassy Creeks.

(c) Low Rocky Point to Bond Bay. Start from either Birches Inlet or Moores Valley and follow the track to the point then along the coast south to Bond Bay where you can be collected by seaplane. This requires 6 to 10 days to walk and a planned time of 8 to 12 days is suggested.

(d) Birches Inlet to Low Rocky Point then Bond Bay and out to the Port Davey Track. This requires 8 to 14 days to walk (time taken can vary greatly according to river heights) and 10 to 16 days should be allowed.

(e) Full Traverse of the coast. Allowing for some rests and delays this will take 22 to 30 days to complete. A rough suggestion is to plan for supplies to be delivered to Hibbs on the 6th day, Mainwaring on the 19th day and fly out from Bond Bay on the 29th or 30th day.

South of Sloop Point

Access. There are no regular services of any kind for accessing the coast and all transport will need to chartered and booked before starting. This makes the cost of walking here more expensive than for other areas. Most access is by the seaplane service based at Strahan (p 27). It may be possible to gain access to parts of the coast by boat and this will depend on the personal contacts.

(a) **Cape Sorrell.** This is the main cape on the southern side of Hells Gates at the entrance to Macquarie Harbour. The easiest access is to get a fishing boat to provide a lift across the narrow harbour entrance. To get to the narrows follow the Lyell Highway from Queenstown to Strahan. A further 15km south-west along the sandy tracks leads to Braddon Point on the north side of the narrows. Arrangements can be made with Wilderness Air (p 27) for transport from Strahan to the narrows and across to the southern side by boat.

(b) **Hibbs Lagoon.** This is a large lagoon close to the ocean on which the sea planes of Wilderness Air can land (p 27). It is an important location either for collecting more supplies or for easy access to the coast.

(c) **Birches Inlet.** This inlet is at the very southern end of Macquarie Harbour. It can be accessed by boat, but is easiest by seaplane.

Wading into Hibbs Bay

The landing point is on the western side of the inlet and it is necessary to follow old tracks south and cross the river to the Low Rocky Point Track. This track is then followed south and is used for access to the coast at Rhueben Creek, Sassy Creek, Low Rocky Point or Cowrie Beach. It takes 2½ to 3 days to follow the tracks south to the coast near Low Rocky Point.

(d) **Moores Valley.** This is a rough landing strip situated about ⅔ of the way down the Low Rocky Point Track, just north of the Wanderer River. The strip is only suitable for wheeled aircraft which are based at Hobart or Launceston (see p 27 for air services). It does save a considerable amount of track bashing but there is no guarantee that the strip is suitable for landings. This must be confirmed with the air companies when booking.

(e) **Bond Bay.** This is a small bay on the northern side of Port Davey. A seaplane can land in the sheltered bay or in Kelly Basin in most weather conditions.

(f) **Port Davey Track.** The suggested route ends near the Lost World Plateau on the track. See p 62 for detailed notes to the track.

Food Supplies. If walking the entire coast most groups would need a food drop. There are two main methods of resupplying food. The first is to preplace it. This can be done by boat or by air. Suitable locations if using seaplanes are Hibbs Lagoon (landing), Mainwaring River (airdrops only), Low Rocky Point area (airdrops only) and Bond Bay (landing). These sites should be fine, however personal experience on two occasions has been that food has been ransacked, once when hidden and secondly an airdrop. Unfortunately this happens to the food caches of both fisherman and bushwalkers. Apparently some of the visitors to the coast don't appreciate the importance of food supplies in such an area.

To prevent a disaster to your trip, my advice is to arrange specific food resupply days with the seaplane service so that you will be present when it arrives. This certainly costs more but ensures food supplies will be recieved.

1. CAPE SORRELL — HIBBS LAGOON   51km

This is the easiest section of the coast and provides an excellent introduction to off track coastal walking. Many sandy beaches interspersed with low rocky headlands provide easy walking. It will take 3 to 5 days of walking to complete this section. The Neilson River is the only large stream which could be difficult to cross in flood and an extra day should be allowed just in case.

Section Times.

Hells Gates — Grandfathers Beach	5km	1½ to 2 hours
Grandfathers Beach — Dunes Creek	10km	4½ to 5½ hours
Dunes Creek — Gorge Creek	7km	4 to 6 hours
Gorge Creek — Neilson River	12km	3½ to 5 hours
Neilson River — Modder River	10km	4 to 5½ hours
Modder River — Hibbs Lagoon	11km	3½ to 4 hours

Description

From the jetty opposite Braddon Point follow the tracks northwest at first then south to descend to the beach just west of Mt Antill. It is worth deviating for an extra hour along the sidetrack to the lighthouse at Cape Sorrell. Continue around the shore into Grandfathers Beach where there is a good campsite 200m north of the creek.

Follow the shore easily south to Dunes Creek. A rough shelter and good camping is found 100m inland beside the largest lake. Rougher walking now leads around Sloop Point to Gorge Creek. Cut across the back of Gorge Point then follow the shingles and sands through many bays to the Neilson River. A good campsite is located on the northern bank of the lagoon with fresh water 40m upstream.

Continue to follow the varied shoreline south to Varna Bay which is recovering from some old fires. Cut across the back of Pennerowne Point and follow the shore to Jones Creek. Walk through the scrub behind the next small point and follow the shoreline around to Hibbs River. A couple of rock faces provide some interest as the bay is entered. Good sheltered campsites are located 60m upstream on the north bank of the river. A track along the south bank of the river leads to the rough jetty used by the seaplane.

Campsites: Campsites are fairly easy to find near most of the creeks along the coast.

2. HIBBS LAGOON — LOW ROCKY POINT   58km

This is the difficult section of the coast and should only be attempted by experienced parties. A lot of scrambling in and out of gulches and some thick scrub must be negotiated in the Christmas Cove area. From Hibbs to Low Rocky requires 10 to 11 days of walking for an experienced party. There are some major rivers to cross as well and a few extra days should be allowed for floods and to enjoy the coast. It is suggested to plan for 13 to 14 days for this section.

The section can be shortened by 2 days at Rhueben Creek by following old exploration tracks east out to the Low Rocky Point Track. This is really only useful if returning by air from either Moores Valley or Birches Inlet. Currently airdrops are permitted on this section of the coast and there is a reasonable site 1km north of the Mainwaring River (about 1½ days north of Low Rocky Point). There are no other suitable sites along the difficult section from Endeavor Bay to the Mainwaring River.

Section Times. Due to thick scrub considerable deviation from the times quoted here can sometimes be expected.

Hibbs Lagoon — Evans Creek	4km	2 to 3 hours
Evans Creek — Spero River	8km	4 to 5 hours
Spero River — Endeavor Bay (east)	7km	2½ to 3½ hours
Endeavor Bay — Driftwood Cove (665718)	4km	5 to 7 hours
Driftwood Cove — Christmas Cove	5km	6 to 9 hours
Christmas Cove — Hartwell Cove	1km	2 to 4 hours
Hartwell Cove — Minder Cove	5km	7 to 10 hours
Minder Cove — Urquhart River	3km	3 to 3½ hours
Urquhart River — Rhueben Creek	6km	5 to 6 hours
Rhueben Creek — Mainwaring River	6km	4 to 5 hours
Mainwaring River — Abo Creek	6km	3 to 4 hours
Abo Creek — Sassy Creek	4km	2 to 2½ hours
Sassy Creek — Low Rocky Point	7km	2½ to 4 hours

Big Seas at Birthday Bay

Description.

From Hibbs Bay follow a cut track over the first bluff then along the rocky shore to Evans Creek. Either follow the wave cut limestone platform or inland through the bracken to Meerim Beach. A worthwhile half day sidetrip is to Point Hibbs. Cross the open buttongrass behind Point Hibbs to Whitehorses Beaches then easily follow the shoreline to Spero River. This varies from knee to chest deep..

Continue to follow the coast fairly easily around Condor Point to the sand of Endeavour Bay. At the end of this beach the difficulties begin with some steep awkward gulches to negotiate. Past these the rocks become easier and lead south for 4km to a small bay with a shingle beach (unofficially called Driftwood Cove 665718). Continue south for 2km to a very difficult gulch. Past here the coast becomes impassable and it is necessary to scrub bash with difficulty, up and over the ridge to Christmas Cove. Cross the Wanderer River (often necessary to swim), climb up into the forest and follow the ridge down into Hartwell Cove. The rocks are not recommended as they

are extremely slow and the final gulches and sea caves will force the party to climb over the ridge anyway.

The next 1km of coast past Hartwell Cove is also very difficult and best avoided. Climb south onto the lightly scrubby ridge. From here many parties have taken various routes to Minder Cove and none were really sure where they went. With magnetic deviations observed varying from 5 to 25 degrees the recommended route is leave the scrub as soon as possible before ending up in hopeless donga. The suggested route from the first ridge is to head south-west down to meet the coast somewhere near a small bay (682664). The shore can then be followed with some minor deviations past gulches to just before High Rocky Point. Climb through the open forest behind the point and descend to Minder Cove.

With the major difficulties passed, the shoreline can be followed with some minor variations to pass more gulches to the Urquhart River. At high tides, bypass the headland south of the river then follow the coastline easily to Rhueben Creek. Continue south for 2km then cross over behind the first headland (717544) to avoid the cliff at sea level. Pass under the second headland, pass the airdrop site (721539) and continue to the Mainwaring River.

This appears a daunting obstacle but is usually an easy wade if crossed where the river narrows where the scrub starts on the northern bank. Continue south for 3km to the first fresh water (737498) since the airdrop site. The coastline is then easily followed to Sassy Creek.

From here there are two route choices. The first is to follow the coast and swim across the Lewis River upstream from the mouth. Here the river is very deep and up to 100m wide. Once across the river it is an easy walk across the buttongrass plains to Low Rocky Point. The other alternative is to head inland across the plains to cross the river at the first rapids. This is just upstream of Stony Creek (789440) and is generally an easy crossing. The plains are then crossed to Low Rocky Point or Cowrie Beach.

Campsites : In contrast to the rest of the coast good campsites along this section can be difficult to find. The following list does not include all possible sites but should assist with planning.

Evans Creek - good site on north bank.
Spero River - good site on south bank of lagoon.
Endeavor Bay - good site on the dune at the bays eastern end.
Driftwood Cove (665718) - good site in forest west of the creek.
Christmas Cove - hidden 50m inland half way along the beach.
Hartwell Cove - good site at the northern end.
High Rocky Point - fair sites at (678659), (674646), (677636)
Minder Cove - exposed sites beside the creek.

Urquhart River - excellent site on the north bank of the river.
Rhueben Creek - reasonable camping south of the creek.
Mainwaring Drop (721539) - fair near the creek to the north.
The Shank (737498) - good site at creek 2km north of the point.
From here there are plenty of sites down to Sassy Creek and also
along the coast east from Low Rocky Point.

3. LOW ROCKY POINT — BOND BAY   55km

From Low Rocky the coastline changes character and has a wide
coastal plain behind the shoreline. These plains have been extensively
burnt and provide simple routes between the major bays of the coast.
There are some scrub bands bordering the edges of the coast and the
creeks, but with careful route selection scrub bashing can be kept to a
minimum. Walking is generally easy for an off-track area. The major
problems are its remoteness and the many river crossings which can
present problems in floods. The coast will take 4 to 7 days to walk
from Low Rocky to Bond Bay and extra time will need to be added
depending on how the section is accessed.

Section Times. These can vary quite a lot depending on how recently
the plains have been burnt and how long the rivers take to cross.

Low Rocky Point — Cowrie Beach	6km	2 to 2½ hours
Cowrie Beach — Pophole	6km	3 to 3½ hours
Pophole — Nye Bay (north)	9km	4 to 6 hours
Nye Bay — Mulcahy Bay (south)	9km	4 to 6 hours
Mulcahy Bay — Wreck Bay (south)	10km	5 to 6½ hours
Wreck Bay — Bond Bay (direct route)	12km	6 to 8 hours
Wreck Bay — Sandblow Bay	8km	4 to 5 hours
Sandblow Bay — Bond Bay (direct route)	7km	2 to 2½ hours
Sandblow Bay — Kelly Basin	8km	4 to 6 hours
Kelly Basin — Bond Bay	7km	3 to 4 hours

Description.

From Low Rocky Point follow the shoreline past Cowrie Beach to
The Pophole. Leave the coast pushing through scrub and follow the
lightly scrubby plains to Elliot Hill. Continue south-east over more
plains to Nye Bay. The Giblin River is very deep and requires a swim.
Past the river follow the inland plains to Mulcahy Bay. The river here
varies yearly from a swim to a wade across the mouth. Follow the
Lower Hut Plains keeping inland from the coastal scrub belt to Wreck
Bay. An good half day sidetrip is to climb Mt Hean if the weather is
fine.

From Wreck Bay it is possible to walk directly towards Bond Bay by following the plains south-east along the foothills of the De Witt Range. Keep east of Towterer Creek to climb onto the ridge then follow the spur to Bond Bay.

To continue from Wreck bay along the coast follow the buttongrass plains south to Towterer Beach then follow the coast to Alfhild Bight. Old buttongrass plains then lead to Sandblow Bay. Buttongrass plains lead directly east to Bond Bay.

The coastline can be followed further south and it is advisable to cross east to Kelly Basin before reaching South East Bight. This bay has steep walls and thick scrub which is best avoided. From Kelly Basin a half day sidetrip leads to the scrub covered summit of Davey Head. An walk across buttongrass leads northwards to Bond Bay.

Campsites: Campsites are plentiful along this section and almost every minor stream provides a suitable site. The largest rivers are often unsuitable as lagoons are usually contaminated with salt water.

4. BOND BAY — PORT DAVEY TRACK   16km

While most walkers would probably fly out from Bond Bay by seaplane these notes are included here for those who wish to walk out to the Port Davey Track. To walk from Bond Bay to the track will take 2 (via Settlement Point) to 4 days (via Davey Gorge) with another 2 days along the track to reach either Scotts Peak or Melaleuca.

From Bond Bay an easy walk north across the buttongrass plains leads to the Davey River near Settlement Point. Here the river is about 250m wide, cold and deep. It can be swum using a li-lo or similar device for support. A wet suit or other insulation can also be helpful. The crossing should only be attempted in calm conditions and it is preferable to have a rising tide. The alternative is to push north through mixed country for 6km to swim the much narrower river near the foot of Davey Gorge. The Davey is a slow moving river and there are no places it can be waded across.

Once across the river at Settlement Point, a gentle climb east along a mildly scrubby ridge can be followed east for 10km to meet the Port Davey Track on the Lost World Plateau. From here it is about 1½ to 2 days walk north to Scotts Peak and about the same to walk south to Melaleuca (see p 62). Alternatively follow the plains north to visit Davey Gorge before heading east over Davey SL to meet the Port Davey Track.

MT ANNE CIRCUIT

Mt Anne is the highest peak in the South-West. With its sharp profile and huge cliffs it dominates the area. It is part of a small range of peaks that are composed of white quartzite capped by red dolerite. This is in sharp contrast to the surrounding white quartzite ranges of the South-West. The scenery and views in fine weather are superb.

With the Scotts Peak Road passing along the foot of this range, Mt Anne can be climbed in a long return daytrip from the road. The recommended trip to attempt is the high level circuit. Although short it is as good as any other trip in the South-West. Fuel stoves must be carried and used as the entire range is a 'Fuel Stove Only' area.

Maps.   TASMAP 1:100,000 Wedge, Old River
TASMAP 1:25,000 Anne, Scotts
The new 1:25,000's are highly recommended as the walking routes are clearly marked on them.

Standard. A good track exists from the road to Mt Anne. Past Mt Anne the circuit becomes rougher. There is some steep scrambling over Mt Lot and it is difficult to follow the track down to the Lonely Tarns. Because of this the circuit is recommended to walkers with some previous off track experience. Navigation can be awkward in poor weather.

Notes.
- Mt Anne is the highest and most exposed peak in the South-West. Violent storms and snowfalls occur every summer. All parties visiting this area should be prepared for cold wet conditions.
- Fuel stoves are essential, this is a 'Fuel Stove Only' area.
- It is advisable to carry a 20m rope. This is useful as a safety line on the final climb to Mt Anne and also for packhauling over Mt Lot. Some parties will find the rope essential.

Walking Times. (a) Mt Anne Circuit. This takes two long days for fit parties, however 3 to 4 days is recommended to explore this area more thoroughly and allow for poor weather. See p 34 for an explanation of the section times - remember to add extra time for stops.

(b) Mt Anne. This is an easy two day visit camping at Shelf Camp and returning via the same route over Mt Eliza. For fit groups this trip can be made into a long day trip of 8 to 10 hours.

Mt Sarah Jane

(c) Mt Eliza. A comfortable return day trip for good views; 4 to 6 hours return.

(d) Lake Judd. A pleasant sheltered day walk starting from Red Tape Creek; 4 to 6 hours return.

(e) Schnells Ridge. Start from Red Tape Creek and follow the Lake Judd Track to the Anne River. From there a steep climb up untracked spurs leads to excellent views; 5 to 7 hours return.

Access. (a) **Mt Anne track.** Follow the Strathgordon road from Hobart past Maydena to Frodshams Pass. Turn left onto the Scotts Peak Road and follow this good gravel road south for 20km to Condominium Creek. A car park and toilets are found beside the road. The track to Mt Anne is signposted. Good campsites are located beside the creek at the end of a side track 50m from the car park.

(b) **Lake Judd track.** This starts at Red Tape Creek which is 9km south of Condominium Creek. The creek and track are both singposted on the side of the road. Coming from Scotts Peak the creek is 2km north of Lake Edgar Dam.

During the summer months, a regular minibus service to Scotts Peak Dam passes both of the access points (p 26).

Mt Anne

1. Condominium Creek — High Camp Hut
4km, 1½ to 2½ hours

A steady climb up an exposed ridge following a well drained, rebuilt track to a good but small stone hut.

From the carpark, follow the track over the plain then up the obvious climbing ridge. The track follows the ridge crest. About halfway up the track descends a little into a saddle and then climbs steeply onto the main ridge to the south. Follow the track up this ridge to the hut which is located 30m right of the track just within the treeline.

Campsites :

- Condominium Creek (480435). Good sheltered camping beside the creek close to the road. Please use the toilet.
- High Camp Hut (511429). A small 2 story hut located in the trees 30m south of the main track. A scenic toilet is located 10m downhill from the hut. Water from the tank. There are also several tent sites near the hut.

2A. High Camp Hut — Mt Anne
4km, 2½ to 3½ hours each way

A very exposed plateau is crossed with tremendous views in fine weather. The track is cairned all the way to the summit and is fairly easy to follow. Parties who are walking the circuit should carry packs for the first two hours and visit the summit as a sidetrip. The final climb is very airy and some parties will wish to use a rope as a safety line.

From the hut climb steeply up Mt Eliza on rough tracks. Boulder hop where necessary to the summit cairn (about ½ to 1 hour). *(When coming down follow 240 degrees Magnetic from the large summit cairn to get onto the correct ridge and the track.)* From Mt Eliza summit, follow the cairns north-east then north across the open exposed plateau. The plateau has several tiny tarns and the views from the eastern edge looking down into Lake Judd are worth deviating to see.

Continue to follow the cairns across an extensive boulder field on the west side of the north peak on the plateau (531442). At the end of the boulder field climb onto the ridge crest (528444). This is about 1½ to 2½ hours from High Camp Hut and is where the Shelf Camp route leaves the summit trail. From here it is about 1½ to 2 hours return to the summit.

From the ridge crest (528444), follow the cairned route north along the ridge top to the foot of the rocky summit tower. Cross the boulder fields under the final cliffs to the right and up to the south-east corner of the peak. From here the route becomes steep and airy and use of a safety line is advised if the peak is wet or has snow on it. At the south-east corner of the peak the cairns lead into a short steep gully. Start up the gully then traverse out of it to the left along a series of ledges. Climb up 3m then traverse back right across the sloping terrace above the gully to the ridge. Exposed climbing over sloping boulders leads to a short ramp. At the top of this ramp ascend directly to the summit. A log book will be found in the summit cairn.

2B. High Camp Hut — Shelf Camp   3km, 2 to 3 hours

Exposed walking across the open plateau. Most parties will wish to visit the summit of Mt Anne and an extra 1 to 2 hours is needed to do this as a sidetrip. Usually High Camp Hut to the Lonely Tarns is done in one day.

Follow the track leading towards Mt Anne to the ridge crest (528444) past the large boulder field. The Shelf Camp track now leaves the main trail and descends a short way down the east side of the ridge. Walk south-east on a descending traverse along the base of some rock faces. These soon end and an easy sidle leads to the slabs and pools of Shelf Camp. The ridge crest to the tarns is a 15 minute walk.

Campsites :
- Shelf Camp (532443). Sheltered from the west and south by an amphi-theatre of cliffs with a spectacular view of Mt Anne. Very exposed on the north-east side. The preferred and driest sites are the rocky slabs. Water from tarns on the shelf.

3. Shelf Camp — Lonely Tarns   3km, 3 to 5 hours

Very rough and exposed scrambling with much boulder hopping, along rough tracks. Some packhauling may be necessary. There are several choices of route, none of them easy. This section should not be attempted in poor weather or by walkers inexperienced with heights. There is very little water to be found along the route.

From Shelf Camp (532443) cross the rough slopes to the east by descending gently down the series of terraces. Initially the track is vague then becomes more defined as the terraces end. It then sidles the steep northern slopes into a saddle on the ridge. Follow the ridge east over a knoll and descend steeply off it on the left. From here there is a choice of routes. The harder route is to continue following the ridge. The easier track sidles the steep northern slopes of several knolls to a ridge providing a fine view of Lots Wife. Here the track climbs up towards The Notch. Do not try to sidle into The Notch, continue to climb until 20m above it and descend steeply down the ridge into it.

The Notch is a narrow saddle with steep drops on both sides. There are two ways out of it.

(i) Climb directly out of the slot on the west side. Necessary for most to packhaul and advisable to use a safety line.

(ii) Descend the steep gully on the south side for about 60m until an exit to the left (east) is possible. Once out on the slopes climb directly up to join the direct route out of the slot.

From here to the summit of Mt Lot there is a further choice of routes. In wet conditions use of a safety line is recommended.

(iii) Follow the ridge crest to the summit. Keep as close as possible to the crest of the ridge. Some packhauling may be required amongst the large boulders.

(iv) Instead of climbing to the ridge top, traverse the slopes high up under the ridge top cliff on the south-west side of Mt Lot. This looks over Lake Judd. Keep traversing onto a small rocky bluff then up into a steep rocky gully. Up with difficulty, then more easily up the screes and boulders to the ridge top 80m west of the summit.

The summit of Mt Lot gives great views of the Lonely Tarns and Lots Wife. This is about 2 to 3 hours from the Shelf Camp. There are two routes from here to the Lonely Tarns, the original route followed the ridge to the east but this is slow and difficult and rarely walked.

From the top of Mt Lot, follow Lightning Ridge to the south. The sharp ridge heads south and occasional cairns show the way. It is very steep with reasonably easy scrambling providing spectacular views. Follow the ridge until on top of a small knob where the scrub starts. Leave the ridge and head south-east along poor tracks and animal pads through the scrub to the fairly clear morainal ridge between the two largest lakes. If the track is lost don't waste time looking for it, instead push on towards the ridge. Follow a track along this ridge east to a track junction and descend to the outlet of either lake. About 1½ to 2 hours from the summit. *(Climbing up onto Lightning Ridge from the lakes head for the small knoll at the foot of the steep ridge on Mt Lot. This is located just north of the very obvious large knoll above the lakes.)*

Camp can be made at Lake Picone or at Judds Charm. There is a rough track through the scrub between the two lakes.

Sidetrip : Lots Wife. Although not very high, this is a spectacular crag and worth climbing. Allow 3 to 4 hours for the return trip from Lake Picone or 2 hours from the saddle between Mt Lot and Lots Wife (553445). From Lake Picone, head north across the buttongrass then climb in light forest to the saddle between Mt Lot and Lots Wife (553445). From the saddle follow the crest of the scrubby, then open ridge, east to the foot of the cliffs of the peak. The summit can be gained by a steep climb up the second major gully on the north side.

Campsites :
- Lake Picone (552437). Exposed wet camping on the plain north of the outlet creek. A plaque to Joe Picone (who died here) will be found on the rocks 30m north of the creek.
- Judds Charm (553434). Some sheltered tent sites are cut into the scrub south of the outlet creek.

Judds Charm

4. Lonely Tarns — Anne River Cable Crossing
10km, 4 to 5½ hours

Easy exposed walking to Mt Sarah Jane, then a scrubby descent following a rough track leads to the buttongrass plains beside the Anne River.

Follow the track leading up the open ridge between Judds Charm and the small lake to the south. A 150m climb south-west following the foot pad leads to an open plateau. To see Angel Falls, from the plateau high point follow the ridge east then descend south to the viewpoint near the falls, about 1 hour return. Follow a faint track south across the undulating plateau crossing the outlets of two lakes then a scrubby valley with some tiny tarns to the south-east side of Mt Sarah Jane. (Do not try to follow the crest of the ridge to Mt Sarah Jane because it is very rough.) Mt Sarah Jane is easily climbed from its south-east side. Allow an extra 1 hour return for this side trip.

Continue south-west to the edge of the plateau overlooking the Anne River. Follow the cairned track south-east along the rocky ridge crest for ½km. A muddy track then descends steeply south-west

Lake Judd Track

through scrub to the plains below. After about 1 to 1½ hours of scrub the track emerges onto buttongrass plains beside the Anne River. The plains are easily followed to meet the Lake Judd Track where it fords the Anne River.

Turn left and follow the well used track south-west across buttongrass then sidle the forested slopes of Schnells Ridge. Gradually the track improves and becomes a very well maintained track as the Anne River Cable Crossing is approached. It is about a 1 to 1½ walk from the ford to the cable crossing.

Sidetrip : Lake Judd. It is worthwhile visiting this lake for the views of the large cliffs towering it. At the Anne River Crossing (530391) wade the river and follow the good track north for a ½ hour until overlooking Lake Judd. Turn east and follow the track 10 minutes to the campsite near the lake outlet. Return by the same track.

Sidetrip : Schnells Ridge. This is worthy of a visit if time permits. It can be easily climbed by following the open ridges from either of the crossings of the Anne River on the Lake Judd track. The tops are open and generally easy walking except for the craggy saddle above Smiths Tarn. The view of the Arthur Ranges, Lake Judd and the Mt Anne area are excellent. It will take 1½ to 2½ hours to climb to the top of Schnells Ridge from the Lake Judd Track.

Campsites :
- Sarah Jane Plateau. In fine weather exposed camping could be made beside any of the small lakes on the plateau east and north-east of Mt Sarah Jane.
- Creek on the lower slopes of Schnells Ridge (519381). A reasonably sheltered campsite on the west side of a small creek. About 30 to 40 minutes from the Anne River crossing.
- Anne River Cable Crossing (498377). A good sheltered campsite is found on the east bank.

5. Anne River Cable Crossing — Red Tape Creek
2km, 30 to 40 minutes

An easy, short walk along a well defined track. Most parties would easily walk from Lonely Tarns to Red Tape Creek in one day.

Either wade, or use the cables to cross if the Anne River is high. The track now climbs west into a low saddle (496376) then sidles south along the western slopes of the hills to Red Tape Creek and the Scotts Peak Road (482367).

Campsites :
- Red Tape Creek (482367). Fair camping on the north side of the creek near the Scotts Peak Road.

From Red Tape Creek, Condominium Creek is 9km north along the road. Edgar Dam campsite is 2km south along the road.

WESTERN ARTHURS TRAVERSE

This is undoubtedly the most spectacular walk in South-West Tasmania. The range is the biggest and most rugged in the area and seen from afar, the jagged skyline promises exciting walking. Some who venture into this range are rewarded with dramatic views of beautiful lakes and rocky quartzite crags that make up this complex range. Others are greeted with the persistent mist, driving rain and occasionally violent storms for which the region is famous. Whatever the weather, a visit to the Western Arthurs is an experience never forgotten.

Short visits to both ends of the range are possible but the real challenge for bushwalkers is to attempt the skyline traverse of the entire range. Camping areas are very limited and during the popular summer months the range is often overcrowded with bushwalkers. Permits and quotas have been proposed so check the current rules (p 29) before planning a visit.

Maps.   TASMAP 1:100,000 Old River
TASMAP 1:25,000 Razorback, Glovers
Maps 1:50,000 p 120, 132, 140

Standard. The routes popularity has reduced the difficulty of the traverse and it is now tame compared to the difficult routes of the south-west. The route is not a formed track but has been worn into a well used pad by the passage of many bushwalkers. The walking is very slow with continual scrambling over roots and branches and many short descents and ascents in precipitous gullies and cliff lines. There are a few places where most parties will need to use a rope to lift or lower packs and bushwalkers. Some of these are dangerous if a walker panics so all party members should be experienced with heights.

The route itself is not hard to follow with cairns, cut tracks and muddy trails showing the way. In fine weather experienced bushwalkers are able to negotiate the traverse along the crest of the range. In poor weather, most parties abandon the traverse at Lake Oberon. Because of the potential weather conditions it is recommended that all parties are experienced with handling wet, cold weather.

Notes.
• This range is subjected to the worst weather the South-West receives. Violent storms and snowfalls occur every summer and all parties

Mt Hesperus

should be prepared for living in cold, wet conditions for the duration of their visit.

- Fuel stoves are essential for all cooking as campfires have been totally banned along the range.
- Most of the camp areas are small, exposed to the weather and wet underfoot. Parties with more than 4 tents will have difficulty finding sufficient sheltered campsites. Timber platforms exist at some sites.
- Use toilets when provided. If no toilet exists, then select an area outside the water catchment.
- There has been much track work in some places. Use the track when provided, in a fan-out area, spread out to avoid creating a track.
- The traverse is extremely popular in summer. All bushwalkers must expect to share the range and campsites with other parties.
- The horizontal distances covered each day may seem short, but due to the rugged, steep terrain the walking is slow and arduous.
- A 20m rope should be carried for packhauling and as a safety line on the more dangerous sections.
- The range can be readily walked in either direction. The traditional direction is from west to east (as described) which places the prevailing westerly winds behind you.

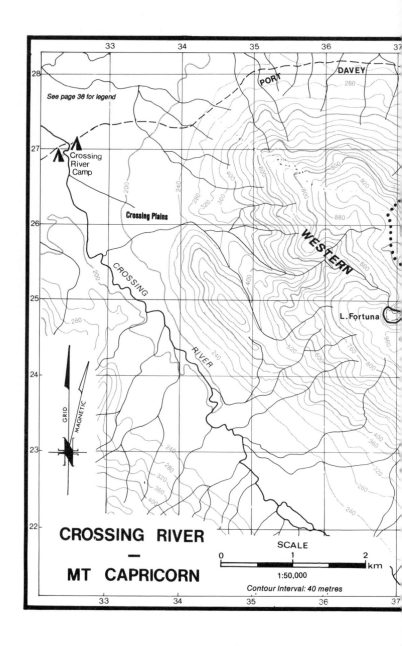

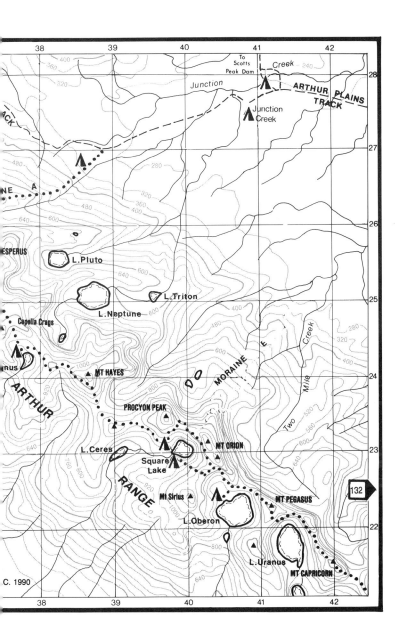

RIVER — MT CAPRICORN

Walking Times. See p 34 for an explanation of the section times - remember to add extra time for stops.

(a) The Full Traverse. Most parties will need 4 to 7 days for the traverse. An extra 2 days is needed for access to and from the range. It is advisable to add some extra time to sit out poor weather. A total of 10 or 11 days is suggested from Scotts Peak return.

(b) Mt Hesperus to Moraine K. This is more popular than the full traverse and it requires 3 to 5 days of walking to complete this part of the range. Adding access, it is a 6 to 8 day circuit from Scotts Peak.

(c) Scottos Peak to Lake Cygnus. A good 2 day return walk from Scotts Peak. Both days are long.

Access. The Western Arthurs is situated 90 km south-west of Hobart. The main access is via the Strathgordon Road which leads to Scotts Peak Dam. This is about 2 to 3 hours walk from the foot of the range (refer Port Davey Track p 58).

(a) **Western end (Moraine A).** This is accessible from the Port Davey Track from either Crossing River or Junction Creek (p 58). Moraine A is about 3 hours from the road at Scotts Peak Dam.

Mt Hesperus

(b) **Eastern end.** This is usually approached from Cracroft Crossing on the Huon and Arthur Plains Tracks (p 54). It also can be approached directly from Pass Creek at the foot of Luckmans Lead (see Federation via the Eastern Arthurs p XX). It is one full days walk from the roads at Scotts Peak or the Picton River.

(c) **Moraine K.** For shorter visits to the range this ridge can be used as access from the Arthur Plains.

(d) **Southern ridges.** Several of the ridges leading from the Crossing River Plains are negotiable. The ridge to Mt Pegasus is fairly open. Access from the south should only be attempted by very experienced parties exploring lesser known areas.

1A. Junction Creek — Lake Cygnus
map 120, 6½ km, 3½ to 5 hours

A long climb following a well worn track up Moraine A leads onto the open tops of the range. Easy walking then leads to the beautiful lakes of Fortuna and Cygnus. Strong parties are able to continue to Lake Oberon in one day.

From Junction Creek follow the Port Davey track west for 2km (about 40 minutes) to an unmarked track junction on the buttongrass plain (388270). Follow the left track to the base of Moraine A, a steep ridge. (The right track is the Port Davey Track.) Before climbing onto the range you should washdown your boots, gaiters and tent pegs at the provided washdown stations on the track.

Follow the steep unmarked track up Moraine A. It is easily followed south-west then west to the top of the range. Follow the marked trail south along the moors and climb up to the summit of Mt Hesperus. *(In reverse, from Mt Hesperus walk north-west then north for 1km to a broad saddle and continue 100m past this saddle to where the moors give way to a series of rocky buttresses. Locate the cairns leading right onto Moraine A. The descent should take about 1 hour less).*

From Mt Hesperus descend south following the track towards Lake Fortuna until you can cross south-east along the southern edge of the rock outcrops into the broad open saddle. This a fan-out region. Climb the open slope south-east to another saddle in the Capella Crags then descend steeply south-east down the constructed track to a track junction. Keep to the right and descend to Lake Cygnus.

1B. Crossing River — Lake Cygnus
map 120, 7km, 4 to 6 hours uphill

From Crossing River follow the Port Davey Track east for 7km to the saddle which marks the watershed between the Crossing River

and Huon River systems. From there descend steadily for 1 km to the track junction at the foot of Moraine A, turn right and follow the previous notes for 1A onto the range.

Campsites
- Moraine A Camp (387267). An overused open site on the buttongrass plain at the foot of the ridge, reliable water.
- Lake Fortuna (372250). Camping is no longer allowed at this lake.
- Lake Cygnus (377243). To reduce impacts us ethe rubber matting and timber platforms for campsites. Water should be collected from the stream instead of the lake. A toilet is hidden in the scrub.

2. Lake Cygnus — Square Lake.
map 120, 3km, 1½ to 2½ hours

Reasonably easy walking following the crest of the range. The route is exposed with tremendous views in fine weather. Most parties continue to Lake Oberon as Square Lake has poor camping.

Climb back up the access track to the track junction. Turn right, and a constructed stony track follows the ridge crest south-east to a minor peak (382242). Skirt the small peak on its south side and continue east to the main bulk of Mt Hayes. Traverse the southern slopes of Mt Hayes keeping up high to pass on the uphill side of some rocky pinnacles. The summit can be climbed from above the first pinnacle (see sidetrip below).

Continue across the slopes of Mt Hayes and at the south-eastern end pass under some huge rock buttresses, then descend a steep gully to a large saddle in the range (387236). Climb the ridge south-east to pass the large knoll (390233) on its northern side and continue to sidle the slopes to regain the ridge crest in the next saddle (393234). Leave the saddle by descending south-east following a cairned route. This track sidles steep, rough slopes to contour around into Square Lake. Campsites will be found near the creek and also on the shelf 40m above the lake outlet. *(Walking west climb north-west up the first gully below the outlet to locate the cairned track).*

Sidetrip : Mt Hayes. The summit of Mt Hayes takes about 40 minutes return from the track and provides grandstand views of the area. Leave the main track at the small saddle behind the first pinnacle on the southern slopes as noted above. Climb straight up to the massive summit tower and scramble to the top up the cave and ledge system on the right or use the easier gully around the corner to the left.

Campsites :
- Square Lake (398299). Fair tent sites with poor shelter are located east of the outlet creek. There are also other similar tent sites on the terrace 40m above the lake, west of the outlet creek. Water from the lake.

3. Square Lake — Lake Oberon
map 120, 1km, 1 to 1½ hours

A short climb then a steep descent to the plain behind Lake Oberon. The route is easily followed as long as the first gullies that lead down toward Lake Oberon are ignored. Normally Lake Cygnus to Lake Oberon makes an easy one day walk or a lang day from Junction Creek to Lake Oberon.

From the Square Lake outlet, climb steeply south-east up the slopes to the ridge top. Follow the ridge north-east towards Mt Orion passing a very large buttress on its northern side. Upon reaching the main mass of Mt Orion (403228) descend to the right (south-east) down the gully which is directly under the cliffs. This becomes very steep near the bottom. Do not make the mistake of descending any of the earlier gullies as they end in very thick scrub. Considerable track work has been done in this area so follow the track and signs.

At the bottom of the steep descent follow the base of the cliffs to the left. A rough cut track climbs a little under the cliffs and then crosses some scrub to clear slopes. Turn right and follow these easy rocky slopes down to the plain on the north-west side of Lake Oberon. *(In reverse from Lake Oberon climb the fairly clear slopes north heading towards the east side of Mt Orion. Do not climb north. Upon reaching the cliffs traverse left under the rock faces and climb the steep gully on the left of the cliffs).*

Sidetrip : Mt Sirius, Mt Orion and Procyon Peak. These are all worth climbing if time permits. Mt Sirius and Mt Orion are both easily approached from the main ridge on the route described above. Procyon Peak is more easily approached directly from the western side of Square Lake. An old route once led off the range down Moraine E. With the new track work it is much quicker to return along the range and descend Moraine A than battle with the scrub on Moraine E. Hence the notes for this route have been deleted from this guide.

Campsites :
- Lake Oberon. Timber platforms have been provided. As well there are also some wet sites in the scrub along the western edge of the plain. A toilet is located in the scrub close to the lake. Water from the lake.

4. Lake Oberon — High Moor
map 120, 132, 4km, 5 to 7 hours

The track now penetrates into the roughest and most exciting part of the range by following the serrated ridges to the east. The route has tremendous views of many glacial lakes yet there is rarely water available along the track itself. The route followed is at times dangerous being poised above high cliffs and requiring ascending and descending steep gullies. It is advisable to have reasonable weather before leaving Lake Oberon as it is very difficult to get off the range until Mt Scorpio is reached. The times taken by each party can vary widely depending on the amount of packhauling needed and how wet the rocks and scrub are.

From Lake Oberon climb easily north-east to the open saddle (408225) between Mt Orion and Mt Pegasus. A small tarn is found here. Climb steeply south-east on rough tracks towards the summit of Mt Pegasus. Some packhauling may be necessary low on the ridge and near the top the packs will have to be lifted up a narrow hole between huge boulders. Continue until near the summit of Mt Pegasus. A track on the south side bypasses the summit tower. This is about 1½ to 2 hours from Lake Oberon. From the top there are good views of the route ahead.

From the summit, walk 100m along the south ridge to a large cairn. From here leave the south ridge and descend a steep gully east to the foot of a rock buttress. Traverse steeply left with caution under this buttress (there are big drops down the gaps between the boulders) then cross steep slopes to the first saddle between Mt Pegasus and Mt Capricorn. A knoll ahead on the ridge is bypassed by descending south down a long gully then sidling south-east across rough scoparia covered slopes to the next saddle. From here climb the ridge south-east to the top of Mt Capricorn. Sometimes water will be found under the large rocks close to the summit.

From the summit of Mt Capricorn continue along the ridge south-east until overlooking a sharp drop into the saddle below (422214). The descent to this saddle is very steep but well trodden and fairly easy to follow. Some parties may wish to use a rope as a safety line. In places there has been so much erosion that the route might eventually become impassable. Descend the steep gully located on the south side of the ridge crest for about 80m until you can cross the ridge to its north-east side. A very steep descent on tree roots and bushes now leads past a small cave (a good cramped lunch site in wet weather) and continues very steeply down the north-east side of the ridge into the open saddle. *(Going uphill the route is visible from below and passes the very steep section by climbing the steep scrubby slopes on the right)*.

From the open saddle climb south-west over the easy slopes of a minor peak into the saddle (426208) before High Moor. Initially climb south up the ridge then follow some rough tracks on the right up through the scrub and boulders. Several tracks exist and they are all awkward. Keep to the west side of the highest rocky outcrops to emerge onto the open moor between the twin peaks of Mt Columba. This grassy area is called High Moor (429203). Cross the open moor eastwards and descend easily to the lower moor. This is the only regular campsite in the range that is not beside a lake, the campsites are the obvious dirt patches. The two steep gullies on the north edge of the moor give excellent views of Lakes Saturn and Dione.

Sidetrip : Pegasus South. About 2 hours return, pass the first cliff on the west and the summit is the last peak on the ridge and has a tough final approach.

Sidetrip : Mt Columba. This is an easy 15 minute climb south from the High Moor Camp. It gives an excellent perspective of the obstacles ahead in the Beggary Bumps and provides grandstand views which are glorious at sunset.

Sidetrip : Dorado Peak. About 2 hours return. Head north-east over the scruby peak, a difficult and at times dangerous descent follows then a final easy climb to the top.

Campsites :
- Mt Capricorn (420215). Poor sites amongst the rocks near the summit. Water unreliable. Emergency only and not recommended.
- High Moor (430204). Exposed muddy tent sites on the south-west side of the lower moor. Some single tent sites scattered around the moor. Water from small soaks in the shallow gully flowing off Mt Columba. This is about 100m south-east from the campsites.

5. High Moor — Haven Lake
map 132, 3½ km, 4 to 6 hours

The route follows a very complex passage through the crags of the Beggary Bumps, then the crest of a serrated ridge is followed to Mt Taurus. A final steep descent then leads to the dubious shelter of Haven Lake. There are many awkward descents and climbs along this section and usually no water until Haven Lake is reached. Some parties continue further to Lake Sirona or Lake Vesta for the day.

From High Moor climb onto the ridge on the south-east side of the moor and follow this ridge north-east to the saddle before the first of the Beggary Bumps. The Bumps are a series of large, rocky pinnacles

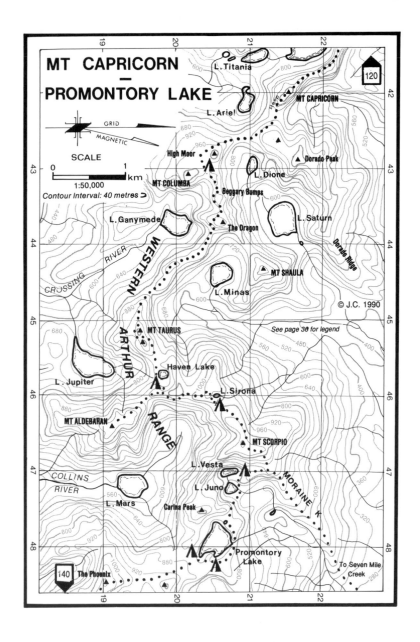

WESTERN ARTHURS :
MT CAPRICORN — PROMONTORY LAKE

and a complex route passes through them. Descend the steep gully on the south side of the saddle and when possible traverse left out of the gully across the steep slopes into the next saddle. It is also possible to climb directly over the first bump and descend steeply to the saddle. Pass the next tower on its north side to a saddle then climb east onto the rocky ridge top. Descend steeply into the next small saddle. The steep, narrow gully on the south side is then negotiated. This is called the 'Tilted Chasm' and care is required descending into it as it is badly eroded. This is the worst erosion place in the range and it is continually changing. A rope may be needed by some parties. From the bottom of the Chasm traverse east along the foot of the cliffs and up to the open saddle (435206). This completes the traverse of the Beggary Bumps.

The next peak to the east is known as The Dragon (437206). The route heads to the right to the terrace under the cliff on the south side of the peak. The track climbs above the cliff, then sidles the southern slopes of The Dragon. Do not climb to the summit, instead the track plunges down a steep gully on the right. The route looks improbable as the track sidles east down very steep slopes to Lovers Leap (438205). This is a 4m drop over a narrow chasm and was once an awkward obstacle. The old route descended the drop and a rope was generally necessary. The present route avoids this by descending the steep gully 10m before Lovers Leap then climbing up to the foot of the drop.

Once past Lovers Leap, descend steeply south-east to the next saddle. The scrubby knife blade ridge leading south-east is now followed for 2km towards Mt Taurus. This ridge has several knolls crowned with short cliffs and many parties have to packhaul to negotiate the obstacles. The route is obvious except on one knoll where the track seems to end on the edge of a cliff on the north side. Walk back 20m and the route will be found to climb 5m directly up the cliff.

After the knolls, the final ridge climbing east to Mt Taurus provides easier walking. This peak has twin summits. From the first summit walk back 80m west then descend the gully on the south side and sidle left into the saddle between the two summits. From here traverse the slopes on the northern side of the second (more eastern) summit and head down steeply through more cliffs to the open ground west of Haven Lake. Follow the south shore of the lake past some exposed campsites. Cross the outlet creek to the alternative campsite area on the eastern side.

Sidetrip : Mt Aldebaran. One of the highest peaks in the Arthurs and worth climbing for the fine view of Lake Mars and the surrounding peaks. Follow the main track towards Mt Scorpio east up to the saddle above Haven Lake. Turn south to leave the main route. Go over a

knoll then follow the western slopes of the ridge south-east to the summit. Allow 2 to 3 hours return from Haven Lake.

Campsites :

* Haven Lake. In a storm, this place is not much of a haven as shelter is poor. Campsites are located near the main track on both sides of the lake. All sites are usually muddy. The eastern shore offers better shelter in windy weather.

6. Haven Lake — Moraine K junction
map 132, 2½ km, 2 to 3 hours

With the difficult section now completed the route provides some pleasant easier walking over some very exposed country. Navigation in mists can be tricky over Mt Scorpio as the track is not well defined across the rocky landscape. The description given here does not end at a campsite, it ends at a major track junction. Most groups descend off the range from Mt Scorpio via Moraine K. If doing this, then continue as for section 7A. If walking to Promontory Lake, follow the notes for section 7B.

From the campsite on the eastern shore of Haven Lake, follow the track climbing east to a saddle on the ridge. On the north side of this saddle descend east onto a sloping terrace. Climb north up this terrace and onto the crags overlooking Haven Lake. Continue north across an open saddle and then climb onto the rocky tops overlooking Lake Sirona. Descend the steep gully on the right directly towards Lake Sirona and scramble under the bluff to pass the lake on its east side. *(In reverse from Lake Sirona traverse under the bluff close to the shore then climb the steep gully).*

From the lake walk north-east and fan-out across the open moor. The broad, boulder covered peak directly ahead can be crossed either over the top or sidle its western slopes. It is best to gain height slowly following open leads north-east. This area has no real track and you are requested to fan-out and not build cairns. After a rough 500m crossing many rocks, you should descend into a high saddle (464209). To the east, directly above, is the summit of Mt Scorpio. Climb up the exposed ridge and drop packs close to the top. Scramble to the summit, take care in windy weather - the view of the lakes to the west is spectacular. Collect packs and sidle across to the plateau which forms the northern end of the peak. Walk north along the plateau for 400m past rocky outcrops then descend a steep gully north-east, onto a major ridge.

This ridge is known as 'Moraine K' and it can be descended all the way to the Arthur Plains. Descend Moraine K for 150m vertically to a track junction. Left leads down the ridge to the Arthur Plains, right leads to Lake Vesta.

Campsites :

- Lake Sirona (461205). Very exposed camping on the plain beside the lake. Excellent views in fine weather. Best avoided if windy.

7A. Moraine K junction to Seven Mile Creek
map 132, 5km, 1½ to 2 hours

Moraine K is a clear open ridge which is easy to follow. Most groups walking the traverse descend this ridge.

From the track junction on the ridge on the north-east side of Mt Scorpio, follow the ridge north-east down onto the Arthur Plains. Follow the plains north-east for 3 km keeping between the creeks. A well used pad leads into the scrub to meet the Arthur Plains Track between the two crossings at Seven Mile Creek (p 56). An alternative route for experienced walkers is to leave Moraine K from just above the plains and walk north crossing scrubby creeks to meet the Arthur Plains Track about 3km west of Seven Mile Creek. *To climb Moraine K from the plains it is easiest to leave the Arthur Plains Track at Seven Mile Creek. Leave the track between the two creek crossings and follow the well used muddy pad south out onto the buttongrass plains. Follow the plains south-west keeping between the creeks to the foot of the ridge.*

7B. Moraine K junction to Promontory Lake
map 132, 2km, 1½ to 2 hours

The scenery from here to the end of the range is less spectacular. As well, the walking is much easier and similar to that found on other ranges in Tasmania. For these reasons this section is not as popular as the rest of the range. Some parties walk from Haven Lake to Lake Vesta or Juno to spend one extra night on top before descending Moraine K.

The track junction on the ridge on the north-east side of Mt Scorpio (Moraine K) has two turnoffs to Lake Vesta. Avoid the upper track as it is steep and eroded. Follow the lower one south into a narrow valley which is descended towards Lake Vesta. Just before the lake the track swings east and descends steeply to the outlet creek at Lake Juno (473209). This is 2 to 3 hours from Haven Lake.

Cross the creek and climb south-east up the ridge to the base of the cliffs of Carina Peak. Follow the terrace under the cliffs east to the open area near a small tarn (477207) west of Promontory Lake. Follow the track around the northern shore then the eastern shore of Promontory Lake to the camping area at the south-east corner of the lake.

Sidetrip : Carina Peak. A 1 to 1½ hour return trip from Promontory Lake. A steep climb up the ramps on the eastern side.

Sidetrip : Mt Canopus. About 2½ to 3 hours return from Promontory Lake. Climb south-east passing a minor peak (485199) then easily east along the ridge to the summit. Fan-out across the open slopes.

Campsites :
- Lake Vesta (470209). Sheltered camping north of the lake near the foot of the descent gully off Moraine K.
- Lake Juno (473209). Small open sites beside the outlet creek.
- Promontory Lake (481203). Poor shelter tucked behind the small promontory on the south- eastern corner of the lake.

8. Promontory Lake — Lake Rosanne
map 140, 9½ km, 5 to 7 hours

Exposed ridge walking leads eastwards to the final crag of the range, West Portal. This is the highest peak in the range and offers excellent views in fine weather. Being less used, the track is scrubbier and hard to follow in some places. It is advisable to have reasonable weather before leaving Promontory Lake as there are no intermediate campsites. Water should be carried for the day as the route is often dry.

From the south-east corner of Promontory Lake climb south onto the low ridge and sidle the western slopes of a minor peak to an open saddle (484196) located north of The Phoenix. There is no single defined track so fan-out through the low scrub from the lake to the saddle. From the saddle a defined track starts - follow it south up the rocks to the summit of The Phoenix (485190).

Descend the south-east ridge of The Phoenix for 300m to where the ridge branches. Follow the south ridge over a minor knoll and descend to the broad saddle (489182) at the start of Centaurus Ridge. Climb east onto this long ridge and follow it for 1km to a short steep descent. The next km is fairly level and leads to a large rocky tower which is sidled past on the south side. At the foot of West Portal (513177) climb south-east up the ridge following open slopes to the rocky crest of the ridge. Leave packs here, the summit is 300m to the south-east - it is the second peak and is a steep airy scramble.

Collecting packs, turn north and follow the ridge called the Crags of Andromeda. The Crags are a series of rocky towers which are climbed over or sidled on the western side. Continue along the crags until the long flat top of Lucifer Ridge is seen. Just before the ridge top, turn right and descend into the broad gully then walk south-east down the gully. In poor visibility, the gully can be easily missed.

Promontory Lake

At the bottom of the gully the track heads east along the base of the cliffs. Initially this is open but the track soon enters thick scrub. The cliffs and scrub above are impressive and it is obvious why the route does not follow the ridge crest. After a slow rough km the track emerges onto the crest of Lucifer Ridge above Lake Rosanne. The open ridge is easily followed east, down to just past the lake. Folowing the track, leave the main ridge here and descend north onto the moraine on the east side of the lake. Descend west to the sandy beach.

Campsites :
- Lake Rosanne (537186). Reasonable shelter behind the sandy beach. Water from the creek 20m upstream of the lake. Select toilets sites outside the lake catchment to the east of the moraine.

9A. Lake Rosanne — Cracroft Crossing
map 140, 5 km, 3 to 4 hours

A steep descent to the Arthur Plains then the flat, often wet, buttongrass plains are crossed to Cracroft Crossing. Once on the plains it is possible to walk westwards to meet the Arthur Plains Track near Nine Mile Creek. This should only be attempted by experienced

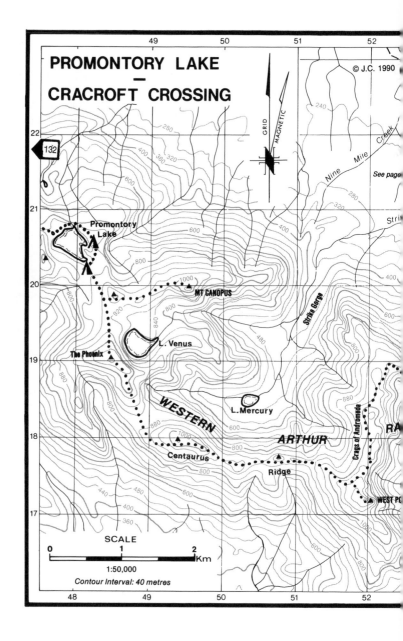

WESTERN ARTHURS : PROMONTO

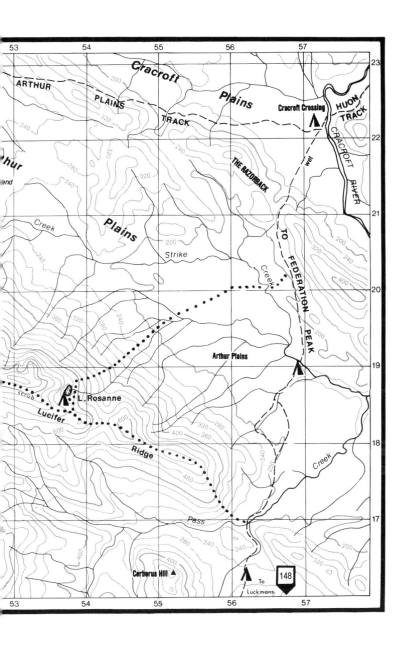

AKE — CRACROFT CROSSING

walkers as there are some scrubby creeks to cross. The standard route is to walk out to Cracroft Crossing then follow the tracks out to the roads.

Follow the eastern shore of Lake Rosanne past the scrubby outlet creek to the main ridge just past the end of the lake. Turn right and follow the track down the ridge that parallels the creek on its north-west side. Follow this north-east down to the Arthur Plains. These plains are fairly open with the occasional scrubby creek.

To go to Cracroft Crossing head due north-east towards the low saddle (567209) in the Razorback. After 1½km of open buttongrass, Strike Creek is approached. The main track avoids the forest on the creek by veering to the right. This route has almost no scrub to the creek, cross the creek and a short climb uphill through low scrub leads to the Federation Peak. Turn left and follow the track north-wards as it skirts the east side of the forest then climbs into the low saddle in the Razorback . Follow the well defined track over the saddle, then north-east across very wet buttongrass plains to Cracroft Crossing.

From Cracroft Crossing , it is about one days walk east along the Huon Track to Picton River or one days walk west along the Arthur Plains to Junction Creek (p 56). If walking out to Scotts Peak, it is one long day or most parties take 1½ days and catch the mid-day TWT bus (p 26).

Campsites :

- Cracroft Crossing (572221). Plenty of flat, dry tentsites on the edge of the forest. Refer Huon - Arthur Plains Tracks (p 56) for more campsites.

9B. Lake Rosanne — Pass Creek
map 140, 4km, 2½ to 4 hours

When combining the Eastern and Western Arthurs together this rough route provides a handy connecting link. The route follows Lucifer Ridge which is covered with buttongrass and some thick scrub bands. The route has a poor track along it that is considerably rougher than the rest of the range as it is rarely used.

From Lake Rosanne climb south, back up onto Lucifer Ridge. Follow the ridge east-south-east over several scrubby knolls then steeply down to Pass Creek. The Federation Peak track will be met just below the creek junction (562170). Follow this track southwards for 1km to the campsites at the foot of the Eastern Arthur Range. Refer Eastern Arthur notes (p 146) for more detail.

FEDERATION PEAK

This impressive peak with its rugged profile and wild surroundings is the major goal for many walkers who enter the South-West. Only twenty-five years ago it was an epic trip for even the most experienced walkers. With the passing of many parties the routes to the summit are now easy to follow across very rough country. The peak still presents a serious challenge and every year many parties are turned back by the legendary bad weather. It should not be underestimated by even the most experienced walkers.

The peak was named by the surveyor T. Moore in the year of Federation, 1901. For many years the defenses of thick scrub, forests and cliffs kept explorers well away. Finally, in December 1947, a Hobart Walking Club party succeeded in traversing the Eastern Arthur Range and climbing up the final rock tower but they were turned back by thick mist only 60m from the top. A Geelong College group led by John Bechervaise followed the same route in January 1949 and succeeded in reaching the summit.

The peak lies at the southern end of the Eastern Arthur Range which comprises of a series of very rugged peaks and ridges. There are two standard approaches and they each have something different to offer. Most parties approach and return via the Eastern Arthur Traverse which is the best trodden and most spectacular route. The other approach is via Farmhouse Creek and Moss Ridge and while shorter and better sheltered it is not as enjoyable. Also the upper sections of Moss Ridge are difficult and can be dangerous in wet windy conditions. There are several other routes which can be used to approach Federation Peak. They are all longer and more difficult and suitable only for very experienced South-West walkers who are competent at discovering their own routes. These other approaches will not be described here.

To simplify the descriptions the notes are divided into three sections; the two approach routes and a separate section detailing the short routes around the peak area. The following information applies to all these routes.

Notes.
- Federation Peak receives some of the worst weather in Tasmania. Violent storms and snowfalls do occur each summer and can last for several days. All parties should allow extra food, time and be prepared for cold wet conditions.
- This is a 'Fuel Stove Only' area. No campfires are allowed.

Federation Peak & Thwaites Plateau

- Rivers and creeks are liable to flooding. Walkers must be prepared to wait if necessary for waters to subside.
- The campsites are not large, so parties should be limited to only 4 tents. Larger parties will have difficulty finding an adequate number of sheltered campsites. Currently overcrowding at campsites is a major problem and the proposed permit system should improve this.
- Some minor rockclimbing is required to reach the summit. It is not a walk but involves climbing using reasonable holds and the final section is poised 600m above a lake. Caution is strongly advised and many parties will wish to use a safety rope. The rope should be a proper rope (not clothes line) of at least 7mm diameter and a 20m length is just sufficient although a 50m length is recommended. Note that a rope is a dangerous item if no-one in the party can belay and handle it properly as it would give a false sense of security. Several people have died here. If you are unsure or nervous do not attempt the climb and do not be disappointed as about half the walkers who reach the peak area don't get to the summit.

Walking Times. Most parties will take from 5 to 10 days to visit the peak and return. This allows for poor weather and sidetrips. The following times are for a one way trip to the peak area. See p 34 for an explanation of the section times - remember to add extra hours for stops and also allow some weather days.

(a) Eastern Arthur Traverse. Approach by the Huon Track or from Scotts Peak and takes 3 to 5 walking days.

(b) Farmhouse Creek and Moss Ridge takes 2 to 3 walking days.

145

FEDERATION VIA THE EASTERN ARTHURS

This is the most scenic and spectacular route to Federation Peak and is the most popular route. A rough and generally unmarked track exists all the way. Care with navigation is still required, especially in poor weather as there are several false leads. Many dramatic views of the peak are seen along the route. Being an exposed high level approach it is subject to the regular bad weather which can make walking and navigation impossible.

Maps.   TASMAP 1:100,000 Old River
              TASMAP 1:25,000 Razorback, Glovers
              Maps 1:50,000 p 148

Standard. This is presently the easiest approach to the peak. It is still a fairly tough trip and is not recommended to inexperienced walking parties. Very rough tracks are followed along most of the route. Pack-hauling in several places is required for most groups.

Notes.
* A 20m rope may be needed by some parties for packhauling along this route.
* Most parties will need to camp at Pass Creek or Goon Moor.
* See p 144 for other special notes on Federation Peak.

Walking Times. Cracroft Crossing to the peak will generally require 2 walking days. At least one day should be allowed to approach Cracroft Crossing from either Scotts Peak Dam or the Picton River. See p 34 for an explanation of the section times - remember to add extra time for stops.

Access. (a) **Cracroft Crossing (north end).** This can be reached by walking along the Huon or Arthur Plains tracks (p 56).
    (b) **Federation Peak (south end).** This can be approached by Farmhouse Creek and Moss Ridge (p 156).

Mt Hopetoun from Luckmans Lead

1. Cracroft Crossing — Pass Creek
map 148, 7km, 2 to 3 hours

An easy half day over wet, open buttongrass plains with a very short climb over the Razorback ridge. Reasonable views of the peak are seen in fine weather.

From Cracroft Crossing (573221) follow the track leading south-west over the wet buttongrass plain (the track heading west goes along the Arthur Plains). Follow the track into the saddle (567209) in the Razorback for the first view of Federation Peak. A rough track is now followed south-east along the north bank of Strike Creek for 2km. This track now turns south to cross Strike Creek and then crosses some smaller creeks. Follow the well defined track south to Pass Creek and follow the west bank to the crossing just north of Cerberus Hill.

Cross Pass Creek (562169) where it divides below Cerberus Hill and follow the east tributary upstream for 600m to where the creek swings south-west. Several tracks exist here as the main route divides several times. To the left of the creek there are two small forests and

147

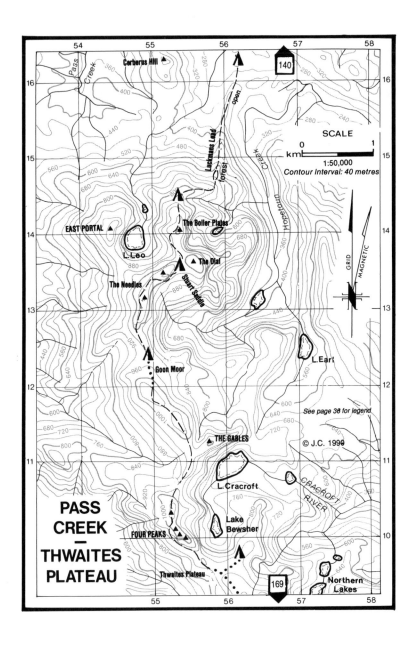

FEDERATION : PASS CREEK — THWAITES PLATEAU

both of them contain suitable camping sites at the foot of Luckmans Lead. It is also possible to approach Pass Creek from the Western Arthurs via Lucifer Ridge (p 142).

Campsites :

- Cracroft Crossing (573221). Many campsites in this area. Water from the river 100m east. See p 56 for more detail.
- Strike Creek (570190). A sheltered area where the track crosses the creek. Emergency only, as it is prone to flooding.
- Pass Creek (562163). A sheltered campsite in either of the two forests at the foot of Luckmans Lead. If the small creek near the forest is dry then water can be found 300m north along the main track. For toilet sites, go downstream of both forests.

2. Pass Creek — Stuart Saddle
map 148, 3km, 3½ to 6 hours

A long, steep haul up a very rough track leads onto the Eastern Arthur Range. Very little water is found on the ascent. Most parties will take 1 hour less on the descent.

From the more western campsite follow the track leading south. This soon climbs onto the clear morainal ridge called Luckmans Lead. Walk south along the level top of this moraine to the start of the climb. Tracks lead up the steep open buttongrass ridge to the forest. In the forest, the track climbs steeply up to a band of cliffs. A very steep climb up the cliffs leads to low scrub on the main ridge. Here a good view of the Dial is obtained.

The scrubby and rocky ridge tops ahead are now followed past a tiny campsite and a final steep climb leads to open tops. Water is often found here in pools beside the track. The rocky tops ahead to the south are the Boiler Plates. Follow the cairned tracks to the rock wall of the Boiler Plates and descend west into the gully for 40m. At the foot of the rocky slab climb up left for 10m, cross the ridge and continue a long descent down the next gully towards Lake Leo. When possible the track swings south crossing steep scrubby slopes then climbs south up to the eastern side of Stuart Saddle. This is named after John Stuart who died from exposure here in the 1950's. His grave is nearby and hidden by scrub.

Sidetrip : The Dial. An untracked climb to the east up scrubby slopes from Stuart Saddle. Views are similar to those from Stuart Saddle. As there is no track, walkers are requested to fan-out to prevent one from forming. About 30 to 40 minutes return to the saddle.

Lake Leo

Campsites :
- Luckmans Lead (554144). This is about 1 hour before Stuart Saddle. Reasonable shelter for 3 tents with water from small soaks or the pool 10 minutes uphill. With unreliable water, this is really only an emergency site.
- Stuart Saddle (554136). Poor muddy campsites with fair shelter are found on the south side of the saddle. Usually no close water; if recently raining try the cliffs to the west near the bivouac.

3. Stuart Saddle — Goon Moor
map 148, 2km, 2 to 3 hours

Rock scrambling and very rough tracks lead along the crest of the range south to the open plateau at Goon Moor. There was once several confusing routes on this section. Follow the signs and ignore old tracks.

Walk along the rough crest of Stuart Saddle to its west side (at present, the track to the campsite does not lead directly to the main track - this is expected to change as track works are completed so follow any signs). Descend the south side of the saddle keeping close under the cliffs of the Needles. About 200m down a group of large boulders with some shelter underneath (the Bivouac) will be passed. Water often drips off the cliffs near here. Descend a further 70m keeping beside the cliff to a terrace which is a false lead. Continue down a further 30m into some pandannis where the track takes a sharp turn to the right (the track straight ahead leads down to Stuart Saddle Lower Camp). Climb up into a steep eroded gully and up onto a wide shelf.

From the wide shelf there were once a variety of routes traversing the southern side of the first tower of the Needles. This was very confusing and also contributed to a lot of erosion. To reduce erosion, track markers have been installed so follow the signs around the southern side of the tower then up into the wide creek gully south of the first tower.

Follow this wide gully uphill until the scrub can be crossed. A short climb west leads onto the flat saddle on the skyline. An arrow and the letters TUMC formed in stones will be found on the ground. *(Coming the other way the arrow shows the way down from the saddle).* The serrated ridge of the Needles is now followed south and there were once several routes around the two crags. Do not follow the ridge top as you will be faced with a difficult descent down cliff faces at the southern end. The easiest route traverses the western slopes of the first crag and then climbs up into the saddle between the two crags. It then descends to the right and sidles up and down passing a rocky shelter to bypass the last needle. At the end of the rocks follow the cut track on the ridge crest south through thick scrub to the open exposed plateau at Goon Moor.

Campsites :
- Stuart Saddle Camp (554136). This was once a poor muddy sloping site but is being hardened and will be the main intermediate campsite on this section. Water is usually available dripping off the cliffs of the Neddles.
- Stuart Saddle Bivouac (554135). This is under the very large rocks 200m down the north side of the saddle under the cliffs of the Needles. Emergency use only - its damp and cramped.
- Goon Moor Forest (548126). A new campsite in forest 200m north of Goon Moor. With timber platforms and tank water this is the recommended site. The old muddy campsites on the moors should not to be used.

4. Goon Moor — Thwaites Plateau
map 148, 4km, 3 to 5 hours

Spectacular views of Federation Peak are obtained along this section in fine weather. The route follows the rough crest of the range and is fairly well cairned along the rocks with rough cut tracks through the scrubby sections.

Walk across Goon Moor by fanning out - this will prevent a muddy track from forming. At the southern end of the moor the track climbs south up the east side of the rocks. Continue along the rocky ridge south-east following cairns over a small moor until opposite The Gables. The main ridge crest now swings south and the route alternates between rocky tops and cut tracks through scrubby patches. This leads past a tiny one tent campsite in a scrubby saddle (553106). Cairned tracks can now be followed south over the top of a broad open peak then down to the scoparia filled saddle (553101) just north of the Four Peaks. *(Walking north from this saddle, do not try to sidle the slopes of the broad peak ahead. Climb directly over the top.)*

The rocky towers of the Four Peaks now bar the way ahead and it is necessary to negotiate them with some rough walking. From the saddle (553101) walk downhill along the cliff face for 100m following cairns. This leads to a short rocky step which is climbed. (If you reach a tall 1m wide slot then you have gone too far as the slot is the old route and was a very difficult obstacle; the new route is 20m uphill from the slot). From the rocky step traverse left around the buttress and down the gully. *(In reverse, 10m before the slot climb the gully and traverse left around the buttress on the new route.)* This exits the party onto the south-west side of the Four Peaks and a difficult route is now followed past the outlying buttresses of the Four Peaks to Thwaites Plateau.

A long descent down the wide gully leads to the first notch between a buttresss and the main mountain. Climb steeply up into the notch then descend very steeply down the other side. Most parties will need to haul packs here. This leads into a gully and a track junction. The left track leads to a very difficult notch which is best avoided. Turn right and follow the track downhill then sidle left underneath the second buttress and back up to join the other route at the foot of the main cliff. Follow the cliff face right and climb with some difficulty into the notch behind the third buttress. The route now eases and passes along well worn tracks through rocks and scrub to the ridge crest past the Four Peaks where there is an excellent view of Lake Bewsher to the north. From here follow the ridge crest southeast to the open grasses of Thwaites Plateau.

Thwaites Plateau provides very easy walking. In poor visibility it can be difficult to navigate. To find the camping ridge follow the left

Federation from the Four Peaks

edge of the plateau for 300m to meet the track leading to the campsites. Alternatively the party can continue further to Hanging Lake or
Bechervaise Plateau. See p 166 for routes to these campsites. Federation Peak can be readily climbed from Thwaites Plateau. Allow 2 to 6
hours return (p 166).

Campsites :
- Saddle Camp (553106). A tiny 1 tent emergency site cut into 3m high
  scoparia. Unreliable water to the west.
- Thwaites Plateau North (562098). A sheltered camp with many tent
  sites cut into 5m high scoparia on the large ridge leading off the north
  side of Thwaites Plateau. Semi-permanent water from pools on the
  plateau. In very dry spells the eastern gully is more reliable but
  scrubby. This is the best sheltered campsite close to Federation Peak.
  For toilets, go well downhill on the west side.

Route Linking : For routes around Federation Peak see p 166.

FEDERATION VIA FARMHOUSE CREEK AND MOSS RIDGE

This is the shortest and quickest route to approach Federation Peak, but it is the least attractive. There are only a few scenic views along the route and the upper section of Moss Ridge involves rockscrambling and packhauling. To some parties these rock faces can be major obstacles particularly in wet weather. This is the most popular approach for local walkers as it is the shortest.

The current route along the Cracroft Valley was marked in 1991 shortly after the previous edition of this guide. The track was altered to avoid an aboriginal site and benefited walkers as it removed two dangerous river crossings. The track is now well established but still has some rough sections. It will not be improved or upgraded and is graded as a track for walkers used to mud, tree roots and scrub.

Maps.   TASMAP 1:100,000 Old River, Huon
TASMAP 1:25,000 Burgess, Bobs.
Maps 1:50,000 page 158, 162
None of the current TASMAP maps show the position of
the re-aligned track.

Standard. A well defined track exists along the entire route. The tracks have few markers and require some experience to follow. The route up Moss Ridge is well defined and steep requiring some scrambling - most parties need to haul packs and it is advised to use a rope.

Notes.
- At least 20m of rope should be carried for packhauling and as a safety line on rock faces.
- The entire route is a 'Fuel Stove Only' area.
- The West Cracroft River is subject to flooding and can inundate the route from Paperbark to Cutting Camps. While it is possible to still wade along the route, there is some danger as it can be easy to fall into the river. In floods it is best to wait a day for it to subside.
- For other special notes on Federation see p 144.

Walking Times. Farmhouse Creek to Bechervaise Plateau will take most parties 2 days to walk. For the return walk along the same route allow 4 or 5 days. Super fit parties have done the trip in a weekend in

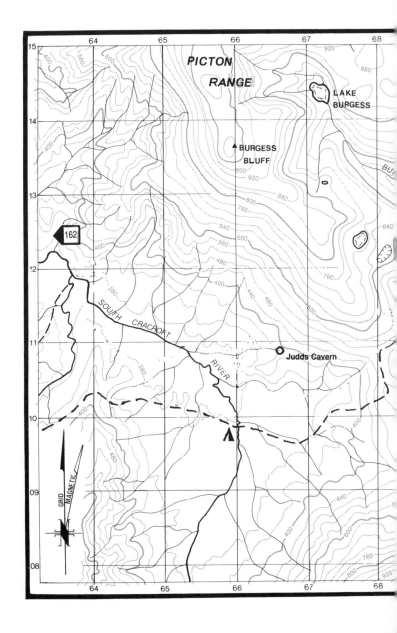

FEDERATION : CRACRO

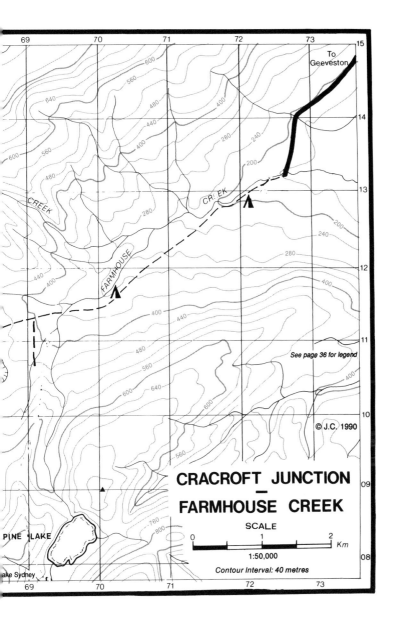

NCTION — FARMHOUSE CK

good weather conditions. See p 34 for an explanation of the section times - remember to add extra time for stops.

Access. (a) Farmhouse Creek (east end). This is approached by road from Geeveston. At the war memorial in Geeveston leave the Huon Highway and turn west onto the signposted Arve Road. This soon becomes gravel and is followed for 27km, ignoring side roads, to the road junction 1km before the Tahune Picnic Shelter. Turn left onto the signposted 'Picton Road' and after a further 1km turn left at another road junction (the right hand road leads to the Huon Track). After 7km the Picton River is crossed on a narrow bridge and the main road is followed for a further 12km to the bridge crossing Farmhouse Creek. Parking is available 500m before the bridge on the ridge or 50m past the bridge on the right. There are several suitable places to camp near the road. Access to the start is by private transport. There are no buses, a charter can be arranged (p 26).

(b) **Bechervaise Plateau (west end).** This is composed of two high terraces just east of Federation Peak. See the Southern Traverse Route for access to the terraces from Thwaites Plateau (p 166).

1. Farmhouse Creek — South Cracroft River
map 158, 9km, 4 to 5½ hours

An easy walk along a defined track which is mainly in mature rainforest. Large trees often fall across the track; they can be difficult to climb over or around and care is needed to locate the track on the other side.

From the bridge follow the track beside the creek west to the registration booth. Continue upstream along the south bank of Farmhouse Creek. Major side creeks are crossed after 45 minutes, then a further hour to the next one then a further 45 minutes to the log crossing over Farmhouse Creek (704122), about 2½ hours from the road.

After the crossing the track climbs west for 30 minutes to a more open area of cutting grass and scrub. This is a very muddy area and here there is an unmarked track junction to Lake Sydney. This heads south and is extremely scrubby. Follow the main track which heads south-west, it soon re-enters forest and a further 40 minutes of gentle climbing leads to the northern side of the South Picton Saddle (681108). This is 3 to 4 hours from the start of the track.

This is the start of the new track alignment that was marked in 1991. Tape markers lead south across the saddle. This passes through thick forest with a very open forest floor and care is needed to folow the indistinct track for 10 minutes to the southern side of the broad saddle. Here the track starts climbing gently onto a ridge then turns sharp right and descends to the west. A steep descent of 1 hour cross-

Mt Hopetoun from Cracroft River

ing some huge fallen logs passes some rough emergency campsites and leads to a large side creek (667096). Just past the creek an area of wet buttongrass provides the first view of Federation Peak. A muddy 40 minutes through scrub leads to the log crossing over the South Cracroft River.

Campsites :
- Farmhouse Creek Lower(725132). A good campsite beside the creek about 40 minutes from the road.
- Farmhouse Creek Upper (703120). Nearly two hours from the road (10 minutes past the second side creek) is this good campsite. *In reverse this is ½ hour past the creek crossing.*
- Farmhouse Creek Crossing (704122). Poor camping in damp rainforest, not recommended.
- South Cracoft River (659098). A good camp on the west bank. During big floods this site can be under water, the rough sites on the track 1 hr east of the river would then be attractive.

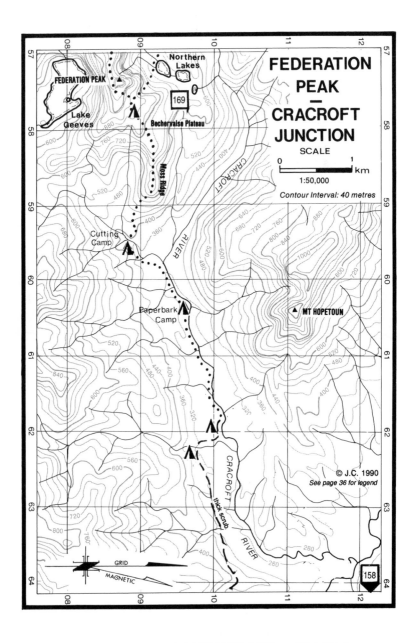

FEDERATION : FEDERATION PEAK — CRACROFT JUNCTION

2. South Cracroft River — Cutting Camp
map 158, 162, 9km, 4 to 5 hours

The new track heads west crossing some open country with fine views of the surrounding mountains then follows the scrubby Cracroft River to the foot of Moss Ridge.

From the South Cracroft River, the track heads west onto open buttongrass plains. Good views are obtained here. The track heads west-north-west for 1 hour across the plains crossing one good creek to the foot of a ridge. The now muddy track climbs south-west up the buttongrass covered ridge towards the forest. When the scrub starts the track heads steeply west down into a gully (good drinking water) then climbs up through forest into the gap (639104) on the large ridge that runs off the Crest Range.

Just past the gap there is a fine view of Federation Peak from a large rock beside the track. The track now sidles the slopes of the Crest Range keeping well above the thick scrub on the Cracroft River (from personal experience the scrub there is thick). An easy walk of 30 minutes in light scrub leads to a creek crossing. More easy walking leads to a low forest and the tightly packed trees provide a gymnastic course. Eventually the trees open up and a small dry campsite is passed just before a large creek (622098) is crossed. This is about 2 to 2½ hours from the South Cracroft River.

Wade the creek, after heavy rainfall this can be deep and dangerous. The track swings north and follows a buttongrass lead parallel to the creek down towards the Cracroft River. It heads west and enters the forest beside the river passing through a large campsite about 30 minutes from the last creek crossing. The track now follows the valley floor westwards. For the next hour it passes across buttongrass openings and through forest as it follows the southern bank of the river to Paperbark Camp (603095). About half way along it joins the old track which was marked by old blazes which are slashes on trees.

The track continues for a further hour along the southern bank of the river (at times almost in the river) then follows the southern bank of a tributary creek into Cutting Camp. This last hour is through scrubby forest and there are plenty of closely spaced tree trunks and branches creating a gymnastic course.

Campsites :
- Crest Camp (623098). A dry but sloping camp on the ridge east of the large creek.
- Forest Camp (616101). A large flat camping area close to the river.
- Paperbark Camp (603095). A large well sheltered camp set in thick forest beside the river. May be underwater after heavy rain.

163

- Cutting Camp (596089). Good sites well above the stream on both sides of the creek.

3. Cutting Camp — Bechervaise Plateau
map 162, 2km, 4 to 5½ hours

A steep climb up a well defined route leading through thick forest then scrub up Moss Ridge. Most parties will need to do some pack-hauling high up the ridge. Times can vary widely on this climb and if you haul packs a lot you might take several hours longer than suggested. There is very little water to be found during the climb. The ridge was named from the pioneers who squeezed moss to obtain water. In reverse, the ridge takes about the same amount of time to walk.

From Cutting Camp, cross the creek and follow the track through the forest. It corsses some deep mud on a river terrace then soon starts climbing onto the ridge. A rough 2 to 3 hours of steep climbing over and under logs in the forest leads to Moss Camp. This is a very poor bivouac site nestled under a rock face. About 15 minutes past the bivvy a very steep climb leads onto the top of a knoll from where there are fine views of Federation Peak. While Bechervaise Plateau looks very close, it is still 2 to 2½ hours away.

Northern Lakes from Bechervaise Plateau

Cracroft valley from Bechervaise Plateau

The ridge ahead is a series of very steep knolls which have to be ascended and descended. This is the most difficult section and most groups will have to haul packs in several places. Very slowly, the track works its way west and eventually you will reach the east end of lower Bechervaise Plateau. *(Coming down, the track to Moss Ridge leaves at the highest point of the east end of the lower terrace).* Bechervaise Plateau is actually two terraces poised on very steep slopes. A short 5 minute climb leads to the upper terrace.

Campsites :
- Moss Camp (589091). A very poor muddy bivouac site under a rock face which is only useful in an emergency. Water unreliable.
- Lower Bechervaise (578090). Semi-sheltered sites with water from pools or the Upper Terrace.
- Upper Bechervaise (577089). Exposed sites with water from the creek. The slopes west of the track linking the two terraces is the toilet area.

Route Linking : From the plateau Federation Peak is climbed by following the Southern Traverse to the Direct Ascent (p 166). The Southern Traverse also provides access to Thwaites Plateau and Hanging Lake.

FEDERATION PEAK ROUTES

The climax to any trip to Federation Peak is to reach the actual summit. Here the log book can be signed and read and one of the great wilderness panoramas can be seen in fine weather. There are several short routes around the peak which link the major features together. Only the easiest route to the summit has been described here. The original route, 'The Climbing Gully', has not been described here as it is a harder climb and is more dangerous with some loose rock on it.

Of those who reach the peak area, only about half actually get to the top. This is due to poor weather and the difficulty of the final ascent so don't be too disappointed.

Maps.   TASMAP 1:100,000 Old River
Map 1:25,000 p 169

Walking Times. See p 34 for an explanation of the section times - remember to add extra time for stops.

Access. (a) **Thwaites Plateau**. This is approached by the Eastern Arthurs (p 146).
(b) **Bechervaise Plateau.** This is approached from Farmhouse Creek and Moss Ridge (p 156).

1. Thwaites Plateau — Hanging Lake
map 169, 2km, ½ to 1 hour

A short route providing easy walking with spectacular views. Please follow the suggested route as this has been designed to minimise erosion and is also much easier to follow in poor visibility. Many groups have become temporarily lost (some overnight) on Thwaites Pleateau in mist.

From the campsite, follow the track out onto the open plateau and walk south-west to the crest of the plateau near the Four Peaks fan-out sign. Turn left and follow the crest of Thwaites Plateau south-east, then climb towards the Devils Thumb. This is the obvious pinnacle on the skyline and the views of Federation from here are not to be missed. From the Devils Thumb, follow the rocky ridge south then east up a wide scoparia covered slope to an open moor (568086). (From here the Southern Traverse leads over the rocky ridge to the east.) To continue to Hanging Lake, walk south from this moor through a break in the rocks then down scree slopes to the open ridge

Reading the summit log book

which is the moraine wall forming Hanging Lake. If you climb Geeves Bluff fan-out to prevent more erosion. If permanent tracks develop on this climb then in the future years, ascents might be banned.

2. The Southern Traverse   map 169, 1km, 1 to 2 hours

This is the high level route from Thwaites Plateau to Bechervaise Plateau. It traverses across the incredibly steep southern face of Federation Peak. The route has some awkward scrambling with tremendous exposure and requires care to cross it safely. The route is also used to gain access to the Direct Ascent Route to the summit. Parties carrying packs across the route should double the times given above.

Leave Thwaites Plateau at the open moor (568086) described in the Thwaites — Hanging Lake route above. Follow the rocky ridge east towards Federation Peak. This requires some steep climbing down rocky slabs and small cliffs. Nearing Federation an obvious window view of the peak between two rocks is passed. About 200m past this view the track heads down a short gully to the right then traverses left under a small overhang. The track then climbs steeply using timber steps into a notch in the tower above then descends into the saddle behind at the foot of the summit block. Follow the cairns east for 100m to the start of the Direct Ascent Route which is the easiest route to the summit.

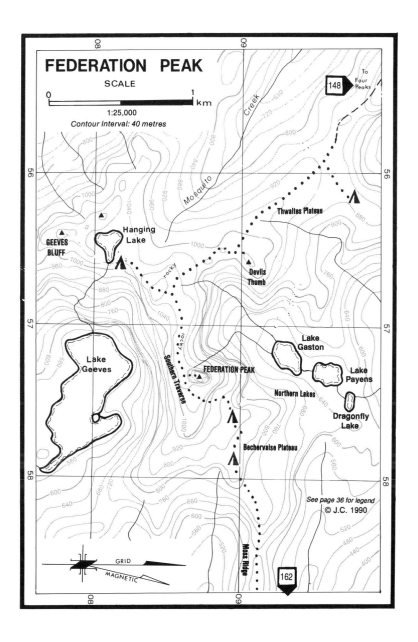

FEDERATION : FEDERATION PEAK

To continue to Bechervaise, follow the cairns east down a long steep gully passing under a large chockstone to the foot of Geeves Gully. This is the large gully which bisects the south face. Cross the gully then climb very steeply with great care into the long narrow gully above. Follow this gully up to the wide terrace on the east side of the peak. (An old route, 'The Climbing Gully', started here for the summit) Walk south-east across the terrace then descend very steeply north down a rockface (a waterfall after rain) then left down a ramp and finally exit out right through the scrub onto the western end of Upper Bechervaise Plateau.

3. Direct Ascent to the Summit.   map 169, ½ to 2 hours

The final tower requires some basic rock climbing with tremendous exposure. It is not difficult for experienced rockclimbers, bushwalkers without climbing experience should be confident on rock. As a guide, if you have carried your pack in along either of the two approach routes without needing to packhaul then you should few problems. If you found it necessary to packhaul then think twice about climbing to the top. The most difficult part is getting down. If you are scared by heights then an ascent is not advised as it is poised 600m above lake Geeves (this is the tallest cliff in Australia). It is possible to use a safety rope (p 144) and if doing so then the belayer should be an experienced climber as there are very few secure places where a rope can be fixed. Allow 2 to 6 hours for the return trip to the summit from either Thwaites or Bechervaise Plateaus.

The route starts about half way along the Southern Traverse as described previously. Follow cairns directly up the slope to the foot of a rocky step in the gully above. Climb this by traversing up left then right up the ramp. About 10m higher up, the track leads left out of the gully across steep rock into the next short gully. Climb steeply up this gully for 30m then follow the steep ridge up right for another 20m.

Above sheer rock walls bar the way. The route heads right to the foot of a rocky wall. Climb steeply up the corner on the left of the wall then follow the ledge right and climb the shallow groove in the centre of the wall to the grassy ramp above. Continue up the ramp into the top of Geeves Gully. Climb the gully to the ridge crest and follow the left ridge to the roomy summit and log book.

The views are tremendous and care should be taken near the edge as it is often very windy on top. In fine weather expect frequent scenic air craft flights. While at times annoying it is far better they are up there in the air and not on the ground. Return to the Southern Traverse by the same route. Extreme care must be taken on descending as this is the most difficult part of the climb.

The final summit tower from the Southern Traverse

Campsites :

- Thwaites Plateau North (562098). A large well sheltered camp cut into 5m high scoparia on the large ridge on the north side of Thwaites Plateau. Water from pools on the plateau. This is the best sheltered site near the peak.
- Hanging Lake (566082). Timber platforms are provided below the northern rim of the open ridge near the lake outlet. Tremendous views but unattractive in poor weather. Camping beside the lake is now banned. Go downhill from the camp for toilets.
- Bechervaise Plateau (576089). Provides the only campsites east of the peak. Both upper and lower plateaus have semi-exposed sites. Water from pools or the creek on the upper plateau.

FRANKLAND TRAVERSE

This is an enjoyable range traverse well suited to experienced walking parties. It consists of a mixture of open moors, rough rocky scrambles and scrubby bands that are typical of much of the South-West. The suggested route follows the crest of the Wilmot and Frankland Ranges which tower above the western edge of the extensive Lake Pedder impoundment. Because of the dam, retreat from the range crest is almost impossible and all parties must be able to cope with extreme weather conditions.

Maps.   TASMAP 1:100,000 Olga, Wedge, Old River
TASMAP 1:25,000 Serpentine, Rookery

Standard.   The challenge of this route should only be accepted by hardened walking parties, preferably with lots of South West experience and also familiarity with extremely windy, wet conditions. Much of the walking is not difficult, just very exposed and as there are no emergency short cuts or retreats from the range go prepared for the worst. The route does not have a well worn pad along it and requires some navigational and route finding experience. On open moors walkers are requested to fan-out to reduce track formation. This has been designated a no track area. Towards the southern end there is a reasonable amount of thick scrub and some dangerous scrambling through cliffs.

Notes.
- The range is very exposed and subject to extreme weather conditions. In poor conditions do not be fooled into descending towards Pedder Dam as thick scrub lines the shore.
- Most of the campsites have some protection from the westerlies but are exposed to the less common easterly storms.
- Water is unreliable along the crest in hot weather except as noted.
- This is a 'Fuel Stove Only' area, all fires are banned.
- The notes presented here are in a very brief format suitable for experienced walkers to plan a successful trip. They describe only major obstacles and leave a considerable amount of route finding to be done. If the notes seem inadequate then it is recommended to gain experience on some better known walks before attepting this route.

Walking Times.

(a) Serpentine Dam to Scotts Peak Dam. A minimum of six walking days is required to complete the traverse. To allow for weather and some exploration parties are advised to plan for a 9 to 12 day visit. The traverse can be done in either direction.

(b) Mt Sprent Daytrip. A fairly long day of 5 to 8 hours return for panoramic views in fine weather.

Access. (a) **Serpentine Dam (north end).** Follow the Gordon River Road through Maydena to Strathgordon. Continue on the main road through the town and after 11km turn left. After another 1km turn right to the end of the road near the dam wall. Presently there are no scheduled bus services to Strathgordon. The best solution for access is to charter a bus (p 26) from TWT or take a taxi from Hobart.

(b) **Scotts Peak (south end).** This is the starting point for the Port Davey track and has a regular bushwalkers bus service during summer (p 26).

Section Times.

Serpentine Dam — Mt Sprent	3km	3 to 4 hours
Mt Sprent — Islet Lake	8km	5 to 6 hours
Islet Lake — Coronation Peak	7km	5 to 7 hours
Coronation Peak — Cupola	5km	3½ to 5 hours
Cupola — Citadel Shelf	2½km	1½ to 2 hours
Citadel Shelf — Frankland Peak	8km	6 to 7 hours
Frankland Peak — Saddle past Secheron	2km	6 to 8 hours
Saddle past Secheron — Pebbly Creek	5km	4 to 5 hours
Pebbly Creek — Scotts Peak	10km	6 to 8 hours
Alternative route		
Frankland Peak — Jones Pass	2km	3 to 5 hours
Jones Pass — Pebbly Creek	7km	4 to 5 hours

Description.

From Serpentine Dam a rough track climbs open ridges to Mt Sprent. The open untracked crest of the range is then easily followed south to Koruna Peak (160540) near Islet Lake. A short section of very thick scrub bars the way to Islet Lake where there is a campsite.

Continue south following high valleys on the east side of the range then the range crest past Lake Wilmot to the saddle dividing the Wilmot and Frankland Ranges. Steep climbing south up the ridge leads onto the Frankland Range. Continue east along the crest. A side trip north-east leads to Coronation Peak and the plain below.

Return to the range crest and continue south to the southern summit of Double Peak. Follow the rocky Madonna Ridge south bypassing the first tower on the western side. Continue easily south-east to

Redtop Peak and further on to The Cupola. This provides reasonable camping in the grassy bowl to the east.

Easy walking along the crest leads to The Lion then a difficult descent south down the ridge leads to the Citadel area. Citadel Shelf is located on the east side of the ridge and provides good camping. The Citadel can be climbed by a very steep exposed route up the western face. Remote Peak can be climbed as full day sidetrip.

Continue to follow the main range south-east through some scrubby saddles over Cleft Peak and Greycap to Frankland Saddle. Poor exposed camps exist along this section. Climb east into the next saddle then easily south-east onto Frankland Peak. Rough camping is available in the saddle and near a tower passed on the ascent.

From the top of Frankland Peak the route descends very steeply east to the saddle below and involves packhauling. Rough walking leads onto Secheron Peak and another steep descent down the northern face leads to the next saddle. Easy walking leads into the larger saddle (320404) and reasonable camping.

Easy walking leads over Terminal Peak and east down to the dam shore. Follow the shore south then eventually east to the road at Scotts Peak.

An alternative route exists from Frankland Peak to the lake shore. From Frankland Peak follow the ridge south to Right Angle Peak and descend through very thick scrub to Jones Pass. Follow either the creek east or climb over Mt Giblin to the dam shore near Pebbly Creek joining the above route.

Campsite near Coronation Peak

DENISON, SPIRES AND KING WILLIAM RANGES

These are three major ranges in the Franklin-Gordon River Wild Rivers National Park that are well known to experienced walkers. The Denison Range is the more popular one as it has several excellent lakes and fairly easy walking across its open tops. While there is some good walking in this area, I have only described the access routes in detail and just provide some general ideas of walks that start here. Much of this region has been designated as wilderness and is being managed as an area without tracks. Walkers are encouraged to fan-out in these off-track areas and not create regular pads or tracks. The best way to do this is if each group selects their own routes with minimal knowledge of where others have walked before.

Maps   TASMAP 1:100,000 Wedge, Nive
TASMAP 1:25,000 Tiger, Gordonvale, Wylds, Spires, Algonkian, Majors, Arrowsmith

Standard. The brief notes and lack of tracks make this an ideal area for very experienced walkers. As with any off-track region, expect reasonable tracks to access the area then you are on your own and times will depend greatly on your own skill at finding a way through or around the landscape features. This area is different to many of the other ranges - there are a variety of routes and each group is encouraged to follow different routes and to not form tracks.

Notes.
- The ranges in this area are lower in elevation than some of the other major ranges so expect more scrub, much of the area is well below the winter snow line.
- This is a 'Fuel Stove Only' area, campfires are totally banned.
- The notes presented here are in a very brief format suitable for experienced walkers to plan a successful trip. They describe major features and leave a considerable amount of route finding to be done. If the notes seem inadequate then it is recommended to gain experience on some better known walks before attempting this area.

Walking Times.
   (a) Denison Range. To follow Timbs Track from the Gordon River Road to Lake Rhona takes 2 full days each way.

Lake Rhona, Denison Range

(b) From the Tiger Range, you can walk to Lake Rhona in 1 day. This is a popular weekend trip with walkers using private transport.

(c) From Lake Rhona to the Spires is 2 days walk for most groups. Another full day is needed to reach the area near Flame Peak.

(d) The King William Range takes about 4 days to traverse the whole range. Several shorter trips are possible.

(e) To walk both the King Williams and the Denisons takes most groups at least 10 days.

Access.

(a) Timbs Track (south access). Follow the Gordon River Road to Maydena. Continue on the main road and 22km past the town, the signposted track starts on the right. If you are driving and reach the Needles Picnic Area then you are 3km past the track. Access by bus is available during summer on the regular bus service to Scotts Peak with TWT (p 26).

(b) Tiger Range (east access). Local walkers have been using the forestry roads in the Florentine valley for many years. These are private roads managed by ANM in New Norfolk and a key to the locked gate is needed. From Maydena, drive to the entry gate 3km west of the town. Turn right onto the locked Florentine Road. Follow this road north for 30km to cross the Florentine River. Turn left onto the first or third road and head east through a maze of forestry roads to an open area suitable for parking on Terry Walch Road (508822). The key to the gate can be loaned from ANM, 79 Hamilton Rd, New Norfolk (tel 6261 4055). A $50 deposit applies, the roads are private roads and care must be taken to avoid heavy transports.

(c) Mt King William I (north access). From Derwent Bridge follow the Lyell Highway west for 10km to the bridge over the Navarre River. About 100m past the bridge turn left onto a gravel road. Follow this south for 1km to a parking area just past the creek. The minor track on the right heading south-west is the route to King William I. Access along the highway is good with a four times a week service with TWT (p 26)

Description.

From the Gordon River Road, clamber over the big logs that close the track to traffic and follow Timbs Track north then east to the Florentine River. Cross the bridge and follow the right hand track to Gordon Bend. The flying fox has been removed so you now have to swim or wade the river to the Rasselas Track. Follow this scrubby track to Gordonvale - the site of an old homestead. The track continues along the valley to the open ridge running down from lake Rhona. Climb this to the lake.

To access Gordonvale from the Tiger Range, follow the old road west which curves around the hill (503818) then heads south down to the plains. Leave the track (505099) and walk east across the scrubby plain to the Gordon River (487110). Wade across the river using the logs on the west side to cross the deepest channel. Head west to meet the Vale Of Rasselas Track and follow it north-west for 3 km to Gordonvale. National Parks have proposed building a new access track from the Tiger Range so expect changes.

From Lake Rhona, do not climb north-west towards Reeds Peak. This is extremely steep, has erosion problems and has been closed to walkers. The recommended route is to climb the more gentle ridge on the south side of the lake going over Great Dome to Reeds Peak. This is also more scenic. The range is easily followed north and south.

From the Denisons to the Spires, the main route follows a pad down the ridge leading north-west from Bonds Craig. Once on Badger Flat there are no tracks, head west across a mixture of light and heavy scrub to the range. The Spires consist of a series of rocky crags in a sea of scrubby ridges. You can walk in most directions in this area and groups are encouraged to all take different routes. Try to avoid the few obvious ridges - if more tracks form then when the permit system is implemented there will be good arguments for setting a small quota.

From the Denisons to the King Williams is the long scrubby valley of the Gordon River. An old mining exploration track passes through the valley but this is becoming overgrown and is difficult to follow. This track started at Butlers Gorge and went right through to the Denison River north of Innes High Rocky. Most groups follow this track but usually end up losing up in places and spending some considerable time in thick scrub.

King William I has a very rough road climbing it to service the fire tower on its summit. From the start of the track follow the rough vehicle track southwards until it ends on the east side of King William I. A foot track leads to the fire tower on top. The tracks end here, the range is easily followed south, a very steep scrubby descent leads to the large gap in the range (277200) then an easier climb in forest leads to the southern half of the range. To descend from the end of the range east to the old mining exploration track is very scrubby. There are also various other options for trips such as exploring the lakes on the east side of the range, returning along the road system back to the Lyell Highway, visiting Mt Ronald Cross or exiting via Butlers Gorge.

Mt King William I

FRENCHMANS CAP

This outstanding peak dominates the Franklin River area and is extremely popular with bushwalkers. Its white quartzite dome is flanked by Tasmania's highest vertical cliffs which reach 500m on its south-east face. The mountain and surrounding jagged ridges are composed of white quartzite which give many the impression that the mountain is perpetually snow covered. The peak towers above the surrounding region providing excellent views over much of Tasmania in fine weather.

The Cap is located south of the Lyell Highway not far from Queenstown. The Lyell Highway (Hobart to Queenstown) provides access to the well used track. One and a half days walk is required to reach the peak and most parties return along the same track. A circuit can be made by following rougher tracks crossing the Franklin River at Irenabyss then north to meet the highway. Fuel stoves must be carried as the entire area is a 'Fuel Stove Only' area.

Maps. TASMAP 1:100,000 Franklin
TASMAP 1:50,000 Frenchmans Cap
TASMAP 1:25,000 Loddon, Collingwood, Owen
Map 1:100,000 p 182
The 1:50,000 is the recommended map being produced specially for bushwalkers. If going out via Irenabyss Gorge the 1:25,000's or 1:100,000 will also be needed.

Standard. A muddy track exists from the Lyell Highway to Tahune Hut providing access in all seasons. The route from the hut to the peak is well cairned and requires some easy scrambling. The track down into the Irenabyss is a rough reasonably defined track. The continuation from the Irenabyss to the highway is poorly defined and recommended only for parties experienced with navigation.

Notes.
- The Cap is exposed to Tasmania's worst weather and all parties must be prepared for a cold wet visit.
- While there are two good huts along the route all parties should carry tents as the huts are often full; the walk is popular.
- Fuel stoves are essential this is a 'Fuel Stove Only' area.
- Parties intending to visit Irenabyss Gorge should carry li-los or other inflatable craft.

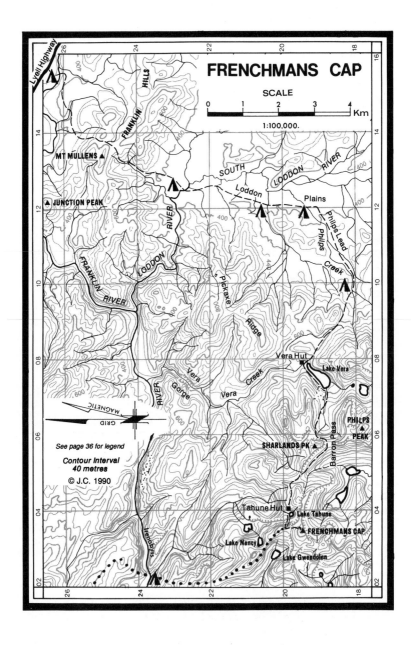

FRENCHMANS CAP

Walking Times. See p 34 for an explanation of the section times - remember to add extra time for stops.

(a) Frenchmans Cap return. Follow the track to and from the peak. Three full days are required for this trip. Most walkers stay at Lake Vera two nights and visit the peak as a daytrip.

(b) The Circuit. For experienced off-track walkers. Follow the track to Tahune, down to Irenabyss and north to the highway. This requires swimming across the Franklin River and is only recommended at low water levels; requires 4 to 6 days of walking.

Access. (a) **Frenchmans Cap Track.** From Hobart follow the Lyell Highway for 173km to Derwent Bridge. Continue along the highway a further 30km to the signposted start of the walking track. A car park area is located west of the track. It is not recommended to leave cars here as they are sometimes vandalised. From Queenstown follow the highway east for 58km to the start of the track. Access by public transport is good as Tasmanian Wilderness Transport (TWT) run a bus service on Tuesday, Thursday, Saturday and Sunday all year from Hobart to Queenstown (p 26). The bus can also be used to complete a circuit if coming out via the Irenabyss.

(b) **Victoria Pass.** This is the usual exit point for the Irenabyss route. It is located 27km west along the highway from the Frenchmans Cap Track.

1. Lyell Highway — Lake Vera
map 182, 16km, 4½ to 6 hours

A well defined track is followed across the plains and foothills. The track can vary from being dry to extremely wet and muddy.

From the highway the track descends to the forest around the Franklin River. Cross the river on the new suspension bridge - observe the limit of one at a time. To leave the river, the track climbs steeply up a long series of steps then sidles east across a long ridge for 1.5km to a side creek. This is a scrub down station for Root Rot - after washing your boots and gaiters continue to follow the well defined track heading south-west. This soon begins to climb steadily through a region of rainforest to the south side of Mt Mullins on the Franklin Hills. The hills are covered with thick scrub and just as you stat descending on the wouth-west side there is a fine view of Frenchmans Cap and the surounding crags. The track continues south-west to descend to the forested banks of the Lodden River about 2 to 2½ hours from the highway.

Cross the river by the suspension bridge. The track follows the river bank upstream for 50m to the old log crossing (it was dangerous - the logs were uually submerged) then heads south-west away from the river. It then follows the western edge of the Lodden Plains south. While clearly defined, most do not call this a track as it crosses swampy regions where there is very deep mud. At present there is no intention to build bridges over the mud and walkers are encouraged to wade down the centre of the track. Two km of muddy walking leads to a major creek and campsite and a further muddy 1 km leads to Philps Creek.

Past the creek, the track turns south-west and follows the button-grass valley known as Philps Lead for 2 km. This is also muddy but not as bad as the Lodden Plains. Eventually the plains and the mud end and the track again crosses Philps Creek in forest. This is where track work starts and from here there is not much mud. The track then climbs west through scrub into open forest and up to a saddle. Crssoing the low saddle, descend through scrub to the buttongrass of Rumney Creek. A well constructed track provides dry walking north-west across the plain to a view point above lake Vera.

A short descent north-west in scrub leads to the Lake Vera Hut. This is located about 100m east of the lake. There are no clear views of the lake as the shores are covered with dense forest or thick scrub.

Campsites :

- Franklin River. Sheltered sites on both sides of the suspension bridge on the north bank - only 10 minutes from the highway.
- Loddon River. Sheltered sites on both banks near the bridge.
- Lodden Plains (121205). Reasonale camping on the north bank of the large creek. The 'Frenchmans Cap' map incorrectly shows the location - it is 500m south of where tha map has it.
- Philps Creek (120194). Good campsites at the first crossing at the southern end of the Loddon Plains.
- Philps Lead (098281). Small sites exist near the top crossing of Philps Lead.
- Lake Vera. The hut will accommodate 20 people comfortably. Two tanks at the hut provide water. Reasonable campsites are located in the scrub on the northern side of the outlet creek. Use the toilet which is located beside the main track 100m south of the hut.

2. Lake Vera — Lake Tahune
map 182, 9km, 3½ to 5 hours

A steep rough track climbs to Barron Pass for magnificient views then easier walking leads to Lake Tahune which is tucked up close to the cliffs of the Cap. If staying at Lake Vera and the weather is uncertain or you want an easy day then it is worth climbing just to Barron Pass as it provides excellent views.

From Lake Vera Hut cross the outlet creek and follow the track along the northern shore of Lake Vera. This is slow due to the many tree roots which have to be negotiated. The track leads to a small wet flat at the western end of the lake then plunges into the rainforest following the creek at first then climbing steeply to Barron Pass. In the forest it was once necessary to climb a cliff but a steep timber stairway bypasses this obstacle. *In reverse, take care descending as the sloping steps are slippery.* Near the top an old landslide is crossed and the track is located to the left as it passes underneath then around the huge boulder. The pass provides wonderful views of lakes, surrounding spires and the huge cliffs of Frenchmans Cap.

From Barron Pass descend west into the edge of the forest then traverse the slopes of Sharlands Peak crossing some scree slopes. The track meets an open ridge which is followed down to Artichoke Valley, a green swamp of pineapple grass. The track keeps above the eastern edge of the swamp and at the end of the short Artichoke Valley the track climbs the gully to the left of the twin rocky towers. From there it traverses rough slopes west to Lake Tahune. Nearing Lake Tahune, the track descends through several cliff lines with the aid of some timber stairways.

Sidetrip : South-East Face. From Tahune Hut a steep un-tracked climb south-east onto the ridge above the lake will reward you with magnificient views of the vertical faces of Frenchmans Cap. To continue along the ridge towards the peak requires some serious scrambling and is only suggested for those with rockclimbing experience. There are several good vantage points on the ridge.

Campsites :
- Lake Vera West. Several wet tentsites exist at the western end of the lake. Emergency only.
- Lake Tahune. The hut near the outlet creek sleeps 16 people. Several tentsites exist in the scrub near the lake south of the hut. A toilet is provided north of the hut. There is no stove or heating in this hut. Water is provided from a tank.

3. Lake Tahune — Frenchmans Cap
map 182, 1km, 1 hour each way

A steep climb leads to the summit. While there is some minor scrambling the track is fairly easy to walk. There is no point going up if the top is under cloud.

From the hut follow the track across the outlet creek then west up the scree slopes to the saddle above known as the North Col. Keep to the formed track to reduce the extensive erosion that has already oc-

South-east face of Frenchmans Cap

cured. At the Col, turn south following the ridge to the cliffs. The track climbs a chimney above Lake Tahune and then ascends a series of ledges to the slopes leading to the summit cairn. In fine weather the views are tremendous and well worth the effort.

4. Lake Tahune — Irenabyss   map 182, 5km, 3 to 4 hours

The Irenabyss, a deep, peaceful chasm on the Franklin River, lies immediately to the north of Frenchmans Cap. A rough track leads down to the campsite at the foot of the gorge. The track has formed from use and is not as well defined as the main track so far followed. It is possible to visit Irenabyss as a long return daytrip of about 6 to 8 hours from Lake Tahune.

Follow the track to the summit as far as the North Col. Turn right and walk north sidling past the rocky crest of the Lions Head. Once past the crags, the track follows the ridge crest north-west for 3km. The ridge top is open and at a low band of cliffs the track swings right (north) and leaves the main ridge. It descends through light scrub and down buttongrass slopes where steps have been installed to reduce

Lake Gwendolen

erosion. The final descent leads into forest and a ladder has been installed for the final descent to the banks of Tahune Creek. The Franklin River is just 15m downstream. *In reverse, walk up Tahune Creek to the ladder and fill in the intentions book located there.*

Sidetrip : Irenabyss. The best views of the gorge are from river level. There is a reasonable viewpoint on top of the cliffs on the north side. An airbed, li-lo or rubber raft is necessary to properly explore the quiet waters of the gorge.

Campsites.
- Irenabyss Campsite. Sheltered sites located on both sides of Tahune Creek (the east bank is better) and also on the other side of the Franklin River.

5. Irenabyss — Mary Creek Plain   7 km, 4 to 5 hours

This route does not have a well defined track along it and is only recommended for experienced walking parties. It leads north from the
river across some minor plains and ranges to the Lyell Highway at
Victoria Pass. It can be walked in a very long day from the river but
most parties will use 2 days to reach the highway and camp on Mary
Creek Plain.

To start it is necessary to swim the Franklin River. It is normally
too deep to wade and should not be attempted in flood conditions.
The best place to cross is at the foot of Irenabyss where it is a very
short 5m swim. Once across the river, a steep climb leads out of the
campsite to the top of a small hill (026244). Follow pads along the
ridge through light scrub, north-west, north-east then north to the
east side of Mary Creek Plain. Camp anywhere, the best sites are usually just inside the trees around the edge of the plain.

Campsites :
* Mary Creek Plain. Reasonable camping inside the forest edge around
  the plain. There are no established sites, you are requested to not create sites and to not leave any signs of your camp when leaving.

5. Mary Creek Plain — Victoria Pass
10 km, 4½ to 5½ hours

There is no single 'best' route to Flat Bluff. To prevent tracks forming,
walkers are requested to fan-out until they reach the vehicle track on
the Raglan Range. Water should be carried as it follows dry ridges.

Follow open leads north-west along any of the ridges to Flat Bluff.
Continue north to the summit of Flat Bluff, then north for 1 km along
the obvious ridge to the Raglan Range. As you climb onto the range,
you will meet an old vehicle track. Follow this to the main Raglan
Range vehicle track and follow it track north-west along the range for
3km. Leave the track by turning right and descend to Bubs Hill then
to Victoria Pass. Alternatively, stay on the vehicle track and follow it
to the highway 4km west of Victoria Pass. The track crosses Nelson
River on a timber bridge in forest and has a locked gate.

Campsites :
* There are no established sites along the route.

FURTHER READING

Australian Mountains — Tyrone Thomas, Hill of content Publishing, 1998.

Bushwalking and Camping — Paddy Pallin, Paddy Pallin Pty Ltd, 12th edition, 1988.

Bushwalking and Mountaincraft Leadership Handbook— Victorian Bushwalking and Mountaincraft Training Advisory Board, Department of Sport and Recreation, 2nd edition, 1986, a new edition is due in 1999.

Classic Wild Walks of Australia — Robert Rankin, Rankin Publishers, 1989.

Safety In The Bush — Hobart Walking Club, 7th edition, 1986.

South-West Tasmania — Ken Collins, Heritage Books, 1990.

Tasmanian Tramp — Hobart Walking Club, interesting club journal which is published about every 2 years.

Trampled Wilderness - A History of South-West Tasmania — Ralph and Kathleen Gowlland, 1977.

Welcome to the Wilderness - Bushwalking Trip Planner for Tasmania's World Heritage Area (free booklet), Department of Parks, and Wildlife Service - this is regulalry revised and the same information is also available on the web site (p 29).

100 Walks In Tasmania — Tyrone Thomas, Hill Of Content Publishing, 3rd edition, 1989.

ACKNOWLEDGEMENTS

Thank you to all those who have assisted in some way with preparing this new edition. In particular a special thanks is given to the bush-walkers who have accompanied me on many trips into this fine region. Without their wit, patience and companionship this guide book would be poorer. Thanks are also due to the other walkers who shared their campsites and knowledge with me, some of them have done this over the internet.

Thanks is also given to the helpful staff of Parks and Wildlife and the World Heritage Track Management Team, particularly Phil Wyatt and Stuart Graham and Tracey Diggins. Monica Chapman is thanked for the tedious task of proof reading, correcting the text and accompaning me on some of many of my walks. Lastly a thank you to all those who fought for the creation of the World Heritage Area.

THE AUTHOR

With 26 years of bushwalking experience in the South-West, John has gained a broad knowledge of the entire area. He is both exploring new places and repeating the classic walks that appear inside this guide.

Originally an engineer, John has worked extensively in both the bushwalking retail shops and as a professional walking guide. Photography of the wilderness has always been one of his interests and his work has appeared in many magazines and journals. He has worked on other guidebooks and is a co-author of the 'Cradle Mountain Lake St Clair and Walls of Jerusalem National Parks' guide as well as being a co-author of 'Bushwalking In Australia'. He presently works as a lecturer in Computer Science.

OTHER GUIDE BOOKS

Cradle Mountain Lake St Clair National Park and Walls Of Jerusalem National Parks, John Chapman and John Siseman, 4th edition, 1998.

The companion book to this guide. This is the bushwalking guide book to the northern section of the Western Tasmania World Heritage Area. The guide is designed for use on one day walks as well as for extended visits. Short walks around Cradle Valley, Lake Dove, Cradle Mountain Lodge and Cynthia Bay start off the track notes. The famous Overland Track is then described along with the numerable sidetracks that exist.

The Walls Of Jerusalem is described with several access approaches and linking routes to the Overland Track. Other lesser known areas have been included to assist experienced parties to explore away from the well trodden tracks. Extensive safety notes covering equipment and advice for visitors is provided as well as a comprehensive address list to assist with pre-trip planning.

Bushwalking In Australia, John Chapman and Monica Chapman, published by Lonely Planet, 3rd edition, 1997.

A bushwalking guide covering every state of Australia. Selected walks have been chosen to be representative and the best of each region. The guide has been designed to be useful for both overseas visitors and to visitors from another state describing the major bushwalking regions in each state then describing some selected walks in detail. Where possible, the walks have been chosen to be accessible by public transport simplifying the problems that visitors often have. The 35 detailed walks cover a broad range from very easy to quite difficult. A comprehensive list of all walking guide books has been included along with a list of brief walk ideas to assist bushwalkers in exploring further.

While the most popular Tasmanian WHA tracks from the book in your hand and the above guide have been included, this book also describes walks in Tasmania to Freycinet, Douglas-Apsley, Tasman Peninsula and Mt Field.